D0494979

THE ARCHAEOLOGY OF SHIPS

A WALCK ARCHAEOLOGY

Editor: Magnus Magnusson

The Archaeology of Ships

Paul Johnstone

Illustrated with photographs and maps and
with drawings by PIPPA BRAND

HENRY Z. WALCK, INC.   New York

FRONTISPIECE
A trial excavation at
night during low tide
to see how much
remains of the hull of
the eighteenth-century
Dutch East Indiaman
Amsterdam which lies
buried in the beach
at Hastings.

Library of Congress Cataloging in Publication Data
Johnstone, Paul.
    The archaeology of ships.
    (A Walck archaeology)
    SUMMARY: Describes some of the
important finds in marine archaeology and
what they have revealed about ships and the
people who built and sailed them.
    1. Ships—History—Juvenile literature.
2. Underwater archaeology—Juvenile literature. 3. Archaeology—Juvenile literature.
    [1. Ships—History. 2. Underwater
    archaeology. 3. Archaeology.] 1. Title.
VM15.J63 913'.031 73-19474
ISBN 0-8098-3532-0

© Paul Johnstone 1974
Drawings and maps © The Bodley Head 1974
All rights reserved
ISBN: 0-8098-3532-0
Library of Congress Catalog Card Number:
73-19474
Printed in Great Britain

CONTENTS

ACKNOWLEDGMENTS

I am grateful to many people whose work has provided information for this book. Principally there are the authors of the detailed accounts of the excavations concerned, notably Peter Throckmorton, George Bass, David Owen, Michael Katzev, Robert Suggs, Alex McKee and Anders Franzen. Many friends, over the years, have generously given me advice, information and help, among them Rupert Bruce-Mitford, Valerie Fenwick, Angela Evans, Peter van Geersdaele, Ted Wright, Peter Marsden, Colin Martin, Anna Ritchie, Ole Crumlin-Pedersen, and Professor Sverre Marstrander. I was fortunate enough to be able to spend several fascinating hours talking to both Ahmed Youssef and C. W. Phillips, and my colleagues in *Chronicle* have loyally endured much ship chat over the years and faithfully brought me back boat pictures from all over the world.

Thanks are due to the following for permission to reproduce black and white photographs: Peter Marsden and Ron Swain, frontispiece; United Arab Republic (Egypt) Tourist Information Centre, page 11; Ahmed Youssef, page 15; Dr George Bass, Peter Throckmorton and Herb Greer, pages 21, 24 and 45; Fototeca Unione, Rome, page 31; the Kyrenia Ship Project and John Veltri, page 37; Dr George Bass, page 54; the American Museum of Natural History, pages 61 and 64; Universitets Oldsaksamling, Oslo, pages 71 and 73; the Viking Ship Museum, Roskilde, pages 75, 77 and 78; Per Simonnaes, Norsk Rikskringkasting, pages 83 and 84; E. V. Wright, pages 89, 90 and 93; Peter Marsden and the Press Association, page 99; Peter Marsden, page 125; Miss Mercie Lack and Henry Bailey King, pages 105 and 106; Alan Sorrell and the BBC, page 109; the Maritime Museum and the Warship *Wasa*, Stockholm, pages 121 and 122; BP Chemicals Ltd, page 129; the National Maritime Museum, Greenwich, page 131.

For permission to use coloured photographs thanks are due to: Dr David Owen, R. Piercy and the University Museum-Geographical Society of Philadelphia underwater expedition in the Straits of Messina, Italy, jacket photograph and facing page 33; the Kyrenia Ship Project and Mrs Susan Katzev, facing page 48; *National Geographic Magazine*, facing page 49; Universitets Oldsaksamling, Oslo, facing page 96 (*top*); the Trustees of the British Museum, facing page 97 (*top* and *bottom*); the Master and Fellows, Magdalene College Cambridge, facing page 113 (*top*); the Maritime Museum and the Warship *Wasa*, Stockholm, facing page 113 (*bottom*). All photographs not specifically acknowledged are the author's.

The drawing on page 13 is based on one in *THE CHEOPS BOATS* published by the Antiquities Department of Egypt, 1960; the drawings on pages 49 and 52 are based on two in *THE HISTORY OF SEAFARING*, edited by Dr George Bass, Thames & Hudson 1972, from the reconstruction work of Dr Frederick van Doorninck, Jr. and J. Richard Steffy; the drawings on pages 79 and 80 are based on two in *THE VIKING SHIPS* by A. W. Brøgger and Haakon Shetelig, Dryers Forlag, Oslo, 1951; the drawings on pages 95 and 96 are based on diagrams by E. V. Wright; the anchor on page 29 is after F. Benoit in *L'Epave du Grand Congloué*.

The publishers have made every effort to trace the owners of copyright material appearing in this book. In the event of any question arising as to the use of such material, the publishers, while expressing regret for any error unconsciously made, will be pleased to make the necessary correction in any future edition.

INTRODUCTION

Ships were the largest single movable objects known to early man. To venture onto the open ocean in them was often as daring as going to the moon today; to overcome the unbiddable violence of the sea a marvellous feat. We can never really appreciate how they felt when they made their voyages. But not quite all of it has to be imagination. A number of the ships themselves survive, and they tell us better than anything else of the skilful cunning, the experienced dexterity, and the strength the earliest sailors used to fight back against the implacable oceans.

As long ago as the eleventh century AD, the biographer of Abbot Ealdred of St Albans recorded that when the holy man had stones for his new church dug from the Roman ruins of Verulamium, his men came across oak timbers smeared with pitch and with rivets in them, half-rusted anchors and pine oars, down by the river bank. Presumably these were the remains of a Roman ship, and this is the earliest account of the digging up of one. Then there is a gap of eight hundred years till 1822, when a sixteenth-century ship which had been found on the banks of the River Rother near Rye in Sussex was excavated and put on display in the Waterloo Road in London.

But the first really adequate excavation and restoration of an ancient vessel was carried out by a Danish archaeologist, Conrad Engelhardt. In 1863 he recovered the Nydam ship of the fourth century AD from a peat bog in Schleswig. This was soon followed by the finding of the magnificent ninth-century Viking ships from Gokstad and Oseberg in Norway. Since the early twentieth century these have provided one of the most vivid of all ways for the

7

general public to experience the past at sea. Now, the excavations on land described in this book and the new scope brought about by the aqualung at sea have greatly multiplied the number of scientifically studied and sometimes still visible ancient ships.

The following chapters are arranged so that the ships they describe appear in their correct historical sequence. But I have also worked on a double shape. Apart from Chapter 1, which is about the oldest extant ship in the world, Chapter 3 is also about the problem of seabed vandalism and robbery; Chapters 2, 4 and 5 are about the techniques of underwater archaeology; Chapter 6 shows how a land excavation in the Marquesas Islands has illumined a sea-going situation; Chapter 7 is about experimental archaeology; Chapter 8 about ancient British ships; Chapter 9 about making plaster casts of ships and Chapter 10 is about the Naval Arms Race.

Between them, these dramatic, if chance, ship discoveries give a picture of the means of sea-travel from the third millennium BC to the middle of the eighteenth century AD. At the moment the record has many gaps, but it is men and work like those described in this book which will one day make it much more complete.

1

The Cheops Ship:
a Sealed Pit

In 1952 the Egyptian Department of Antiquities decided to clear the ground to the east of the Great Pyramid at Giza, preparatory to building a new road round the Pyramids. It was a routine operation, and perhaps the last thing that anyone expected was that it would have such repercussions that the early history of maritime archaeology would need to be rewritten.

A number of boat-shaped pits lie open in the rock round the Great Pyramid and it has always been supposed that they once held ships, to take the dead Pharaoh Cheops, the occupant of the tomb in the Great Pyramid, on his last ceremonial voyages nearly five thousand years ago. In fact, in the nineteen twenties, when one of these was cleared of sand and rubble, fragments of rope and gilded wood were found at the bottom. But it was generally assumed that any other actual ships which might have been deposited round the Pyramid had long since disappeared.

By 1954 the road-building work had revealed the original enclosure wall of the Great Pyramid, its rubble masonry in ruins with no traces of the white plaster which originally had given it a handsome finish. Under this ruined enclosure wall were found some huge limestone blocks, set close to each other in an even row. On May 26th 1954 archaeologists made a small hole by chipping away the end of one of the central blocks. Through this hole they saw an astonishing sight—under the blocks was a pit which was occupied by the dismantled remains of a great wooden ship. On top, spattered by pieces of the plaster that had sealed the blocks and the ruins of a reed mat, could be seen a steering oar, planks, wooden columns with lotus capitals, and bundles of ropes.

OPPOSITE
The dismantled
Cheops ship, lying in
the pit in its thirteen
overlapping layers,
shortly after it had
first been found.

With much care and excitement all the limestone blocks, each weighing fifteen to twenty tons, were lifted away to reveal the full details of this remarkable find. In the pit something of the original shape of the vessel could now be seen, even though it had been taken apart and laid there in thirteen overlapping layers, around 2600 BC. What is more, thanks to the plaster which had sealed the blocks above the pit, the atmosphere inside had retained almost exactly the right humidity to preserve the wood and the ropes in their original state.

Next began the very difficult task of recording, lifting and conserving the 1,224 separate parts of the vessel. A laboratory for treating the wood with polyvinyl acetate was built alongside the pit, and an elaborate system of scaffolding was put over it so that when the photographic record was complete, each piece could be lifted in turn. This took two years.

Then, in 1957, Ahmed Youssef, Egypt's chief restorer, was faced with the task of rebuilding what was by far the oldest surviving ship in the world. For every piece he completed a card with a photograph and full details. Then, with the recording done, he set about the reconstruction. He was helped in this by a fortunate practice of the ancient Egyptian shipbuilders. They had divided the craft into four quarters, and every piece in each quarter had its own carpenter's mark on it. In addition, every two adjoining pieces had two further matching marks. So once having discovered the key to this nautical crossword, Ahmed Youssef at least knew which pieces went together. The wood was examined by the Forest Products Research Laboratory at Princes Risborough in Buckinghamshire, England. They found that while local Egyptian woods like acacia, hop hornbeam, juniper and soapberry were used for some of the smaller parts, the majority of pieces, including the massive side planks which were up to sixty feet long, were of cedar of Lebanon. From very early on, it was clear that the wooden parts had been fastened together not by metal, which was entirely absent from the construction apart from a few copper staples and eyebolts, but by wooden dowels in the thickness of adjoining strakes and by lashings. Hundreds and hundreds of yards of rope, made from the same halfa grass (*Desmostachya bipinnata*) that Egyptians use for rope-making to this day, held those 1,224 parts together. In fact, Ahmed Youssef was able to tell that the ship was not simply made for the one last sacred voyage of the Pharaoh Cheops, but had made a number of voyages—because the lashings,

The original carpenters' marks on the four sections of the boat.

as they became wet and shrank, had cut into the wood and left their marks there. He was also able to make a catalogue of the different types of knots the builders and riggers used: between twenty and thirty, some of them extremely intricate.

Gradually in the course of fourteen years the craft grew and took shape. Ahmed Youssef produced five versions in all before he was finally satisfied.

In its restored form it displaces forty tons, and the bow and stern tower a tremendous twenty-five feet (7·6 metres) above the keel line, while its length overall is just under 140 feet (43 metres). Although it is nearly five thousand years old, this craft is twice as long as Christopher Columbus' *Santa Maria*.

Because tomb paintings and models are usually short of detail about construction methods, the Cheops ship answered many questions. It was flat-bottomed, and had no keel; keels did not appear in Egypt until the New Kingdom (sixteenth to eleventh centuries BC), when they may have been introduced by foreign ship-workers. But nevertheless one authority at least had argued that the 'spine' of a ship, mentioned in a version of the great Egyptian religious work, *The Book of the Dead*, must mean a keel, even if there were no surviving examples. The Cheops ship explained what this 'spine' was: it was in fact a long central shelf running along under the deck beams supported by stanchions. These stanchions rested on sixteen great curved frames.

Everything about the construction, even some of the smaller details, was ingenious. The cabin on deck, for instance, had a projecting frame over its wooden panels, so that a cloth laid over this would produce an insulating layer of air to protect the occupants from the heat. Altogether the Cheops ship was an achievement remarkable for its strength, sophistication and grace. It is impossible to believe that it was a new-fangled piece of work. Centuries of development must have lain behind it.

This is hardly surprising, since Egypt is commonly and rightly called the gift of the Nile. Not only did the river's annual floods provide the basis for the country's economy, it was also the great highway which made the unification and administration of ancient Egypt possible. Everyone possessed a boat who could, and ferrying a poor man across the river was a commonly-quoted charitable action. In these circumstances, the ancient Egyptians were bound to become highly concerned with boats, and very early on another particular local factor also had an important effect. In Egypt, the

The fully restored outline of the Cheops ship.

prevailing wind is to the south, while the Nile of course flows north. In the British Museum there is a large pottery jar of the fourth millennium BC which reflects the early impact of this fact. It shows a boat with sharply upturned ends above a wavy patch of water, and in the boat a mast with an unmistakable if faded sail. This is generally held to be the earliest known representation of the sail. There are some even earlier pots which may show how the idea was evolved. The boats on these have standing on their decks what might be cabins or shrines and as well, in some cases, poles with banners or shields on them. It is not possible to tell what ritual reasons inspired these objects, but one can guess that the helping effect of the shields on poles might have been noticed when going upstream and thus have inspired an invention which was to be crucial to mankind over the next five and a half millennia.

Anyway, by a very early period the ancient Egyptian hieroglyph for 'to go downstream' showed a drifting ship with no mast, like the Cheops ship which is presumed to have been for the downstream part of the dead Pharaoh's ritual last voyage, while the hieroglyph for 'to go upstream' was a ship with a mast and sail. Next to the pit where the Cheops ship was found there is another row of huge limestone blocks, and it is reasonable to suppose that the Pharaoh's 'upstream' sailing ship may also lie there dismantled.

Until the Cheops ship was found, the oldest known ships were the six that were found near the pyramid of Sesostris III at Dahshur in 1893. Three of them were reasonably well preserved and can still be seen today, one in the Field Museum of Natural History in Chicago, the other two in the Cairo Museum. These seemed to fit very well a description by the Greek historian Herodotus of Egyptian craft: 'The boats in which they carry cargo are made of acacia. From this tree they cut logs of two cubits length and put them together like bricks in a wall.' But now we know about the splendid Cheops ship, it is rather puzzling why Sesostris III, one of the most powerful Pharaohs of the Middle Kingdom (c. 2080–

c. 1786 BC), should have had such crude and indifferent craft to carry him on his last journey. Perhaps in fact they were intended for some less distinguished person, plenty of whom lie buried around the Dahshur pyramid.

The difference between these craft and the Cheops ship underlines one perpetual problem of the ancient Egyptian shipbuilders—their need for the magnificently long and strong timbers provided by the cedars of Lebanon. As early as the Thinite period, about 3000 BC, there are references, on a carved wooden plate, to Lebanon and Meru wood and representations of what may be early cargo vessels. When cedar of Lebanon was not available and he had to use short lengths of local wood, the Egyptian shipbuilder was in difficulties. One way he used to overcome this is shown in a painted shipbuilding scene in the recently found tomb of the courtier Nefer, just near the Unas causeway at Saqqara. This shows a rope truss, running from bow to stern over a forked prop, being tightened by twisting a stick which is pushed through the strands of the rope. In the case of a relatively small boat like this, the rope may merely have been a device to maintain the curved shape while the cross-beams and deckbeams were put in position; but in later and larger sea-going craft, this 'hogging truss', as it is called, is a characteristic feature of Egyptian ships, as it was of certain Greek and Roman and even Chinese craft. Where a vessel lacked a stout keel, or even was just too long for the strength of its parts, then this rope held it together and stopped it sagging out of shape.

As well as revealing details of the ships themselves, archaeology can also bring us close to the sailors who manned them. Various texts that have been found on excavated papyri describe the sailor's life very convincingly.

'I had ventured out onto the big green in a ship 120 cubits long and forty cubits broad. One hundred and twenty of Egypt's best sailors were on board. They looked to the sky, they looked to the land, and their heart was braver than the lion's. They foresaw a storm before it had come, and a tempest before it struck.'

The mutterings of the lower deck also come clearly across the centuries.

'The sailor is worn out, the oar in his hand, the lash on his back and his belly empty of food, while the scribe sits in the cabin, the children of the great row him, and there is no reckoning of taxes due from him.'

Ahmed Youssef
(*right*), the restorer of
the Cheops ship,
standing on the cabin
of the vessel as its
restoration nears
completion.

Even more poignant perhaps are the actual sailors' garments that
have survived. There are some in the British Museum, and the
Boston Museum of Fine Arts has a particularly good one from the
tomb in Luxor of Mai-her-peri, the Pharaoh's Fan-bearer. They
consist of loin cloths which appear to be of netting, but in fact are
finely cut from a piece of leather with a central square left solid to
take the rub of the seat when rowing. They may seem rather unlikely
garments at first sight, but a number of tomb paintings of ship's
crews confirm that they were in fact the standard wear.

Other more unlikely ancient Egyptian remains also fill in the
picture of sailors' lives then. When one walks up to the Temple of
Medinet-Habu on the west bank at Thebes for the first time, one is
hardly likely to be thinking of Salamis and Lepanto, Trafalgar and
Jutland. Yet there, recorded on the side of the temple for the first
time, is an aspect of a sailor's life that was to become all too familiar
to later generations—a sea battle. This one was the so-called 'battle
with the Sea Peoples' which took place about 1190 BC, when
Rameses III repulsed an invasion by these people of the sea.

But even more important than any sea victory is a maritime

achievement recorded in the nearby temple of Deir-el-Bahari. Here a now battered relief shows perhaps the most remarkable single craft of antiquity. This is the great barge which in about 1500 BC brought Queen Hatshepsut's obelisks, hewn in one single solid piece of red granite, from the quarries at Aswan 133 miles down river to Thebes. In the relief two obelisks are shown placed end to end on the barge, but some authorities believe this was an artistic convention to show the number of the obelisks, and that they had actually lain side by side. Originally each of the obelisks was thought to weigh only some 350 tons, but the surviving pieces and a newly-found text now seem to show that the obelisks, which were destroyed by Hatshepsut's successor, had in fact been 57 metres high and weighed about 2,400 tons. Using this figure as a basis, it has been calculated that the barge with cargo must have displaced 7,500 tons, a fantastic figure which would make it far and away the largest vessel built until Brunel's *Great Britain* of 1843. There are so many unknown factors in the calculation that this figure has to be taken as an inspired guess, but it is quite certain that the obelisks did come from Aswan and the relief shows thirty rowing tugs hauling the huge craft downstream. Since we now know that the ancient Egyptians were capable of building a vessel like the Cheops ship by 2600 BC, perhaps by 1500 BC they had become capable of this even greater achievement.

2

Cape Gelidonya: Captain Kemal's Spearhead

In 1960 the YMCA swimming class in Philadelphia, USA, acquired a rather unusual recruit. He was a young archaeologist from the University Museum of Pennsylvania and his name was George Bass. Later on, he was to write a book very carefully called *Archaeology Underwater*, not *Underwater Archaeology*, for, as he said, people excavate in jungles and deserts, but do not call it jungle or desert archaeology. In between his swimming class and the publication of *Archaeology Underwater*, he was responsible for a great turning-point in the subject with which his book was concerned.

This was not a new discipline when Bass was recruited to it. Some would say the start was in AD 1535, when Francesco Demarchi, using a wooden diving helmet with a crystal plate, measured one of the Roman Emperor Caligula's great pleasure barges which had sunk to the bottom of Lake Nemi in Italy. Others would give the honour to the English brothers Deane who made accurate drawings in 1832 of objects from the *Royal George* which had turned turtle so disastrously off Spithead in 1786. More often, the year 1900 is made the conventional starting point, when a Greek sponge-diver called Elias Stadiatis returned pale and shaking to the surface from the sea-bed 180 feet down off Cape Antikythera in the Dodecanese Islands. At first his companions thought he had an attack of the 'bends', common enough then. But there was no sign of paralysis. He just kept shaking his head in astonishment as he sat on the deck. At last a stiff dose of Greek brandy induced him to speak. 'Women,' he said. 'Beautiful women—with syphilis!' What he had actually seen on the sea bottom was part of the battered and pock-marked cargo of a first-century BC Roman ship which had been

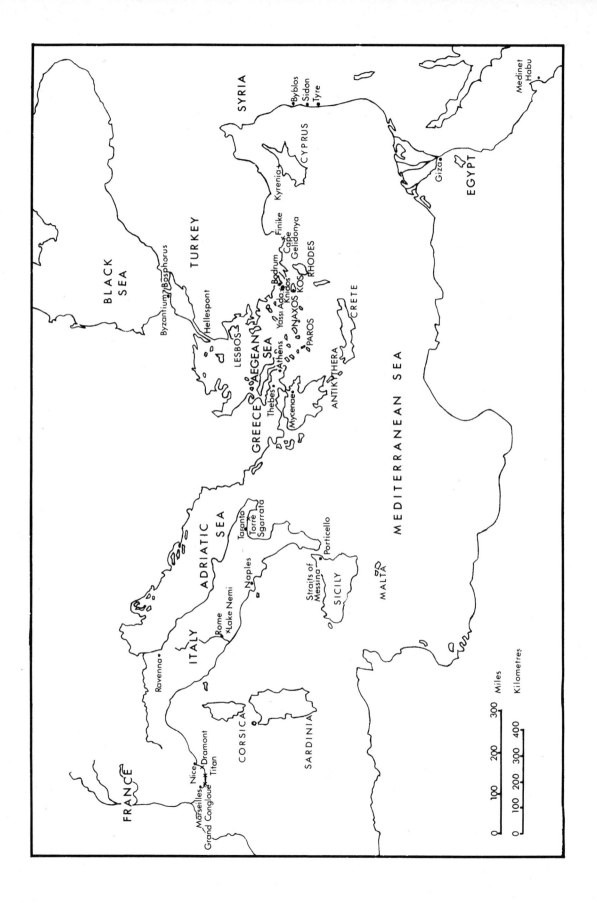

taking bronze and marble statues from Greece to Rome. From this find came the famous statue 'Youth', thought probably to be a bronze by the last great classical Greek sculptor, Lysippos, and also a remarkable astronomical computer in bronze. This mechanism of dials, plates and gear-wheels has been described as the only truly scientific instrument surviving from classical times, other than the simplest measuring devices, and one whose existence we would never have expected merely from written sources.

When Elias Stadiatis and the other sponge-divers of Captain Kondos' crew made these finds, they were wearing copper helmets, lead weights and steel-soled shoes, with air supplied by a hand-cranked compressor. They worked for five minutes at a time 180 feet (55 metres) down, suffering inevitably at that depth from nitrogen narcosis or poisoning, doing a job which virtually no one had ever attempted before. As Peter Throckmorton, one of the pioneers of marine archaeology, has said, it was as if Tutankhamun's tomb had been excavated in five-minute shifts by drunken stevedores wearing coal-scuttles on their heads and never having seen an Egyptian tomb in their lives before.

The device that completely changed the possibilities of this sort of operation was evolved during the German occupation of France in the Second World War. A French naval officer, Jacques-Yves Cousteau, got an engineer, Emile Gagnan, to adapt for use with the Le Prieur diving apparatus an air-regulating device used in wartime wood-burning gas-driven car engines. Thus was born the aqualung, the device which by freeing the diver from all the heavy and elaborate equipment of the hard-helmet era inspired the first great turning-point in archaeology underwater.

To start with, not all the repercussions of the aqualung were favourable. A large number of Mediterranean wrecks were looted by amateur divers, the information embodied in them being lost to science for ever. Even in controlled excavations, the aqualung tended to appeal to sportsmen rather than archaeologists, who were not at first tempted to study the new sea-bed finds in their original position. Nevertheless the sites of the ships explored during this stage, mostly early Roman ones, form the battle honours of the first underwater archaeology campaigns—Grand Congloué, Dramont, Mahdia, Titan, Chrétienne and Albenga. While much useful experience was gained, it was at the expense of much potential knowledge, as the now shrunken and rotting timbers of the Titan wreck confirm. Of his work on this wreck, Commander

The wreck sites of the Mediterranean.

19

Tailliez wrote: 'We have tried sincerely to the best of our ability but I know that many mistakes were made . . . if we had been assisted in the beginning by an archaeologist, he would surely have noted with much greater accuracy the position of each object.'

By 1958, the time when such a situation would be the exception rather than the rule was at last approaching. In that year, Peter Throckmorton, then a journalist with diving and excavating experience, now Assistant Curator of the San Francisco Maritime Museum, arrived in Turkey. He made friends with the sponge-divers, who knew the sea-bed like the backs of their hands, and over innumerable glasses of raki he learnt of the mounds of amphorae which were the commonest signs of ancient wrecks on the sea-bed. He had chosen Bodrum in southern Turkey as his base, both because it was the sponge metropolis of Turkey and also because it was there that Ahmet Erbin, the captain of a sponge trawler, had dragged up in his nets a fourth-century BC bronze bust of the goddess Demeter. From Bodrum, Throckmorton sailed with his chief informant and friend, Captain Kemal Aras, on a series of trips to examine and photograph these shipwreck sites; and it was from Captain Kemal that he heard of another site, too far away to visit immediately, which sounded particularly exciting. From this site, Captain Kemal had brought up a bronze spearhead which was very corroded. He had also lifted a bronze box which he had broken open but thrown away when he found it empty. He had seen several other pieces of badly corroded bronze on the bottom, but they were so stuck together that they could not be moved, and Captain Kemal planned to dynamite the bronze for scrap when he could get there next spring.

Throckmorton managed to dissuade him from this plan, and instead got him to record the position of the site as accurately as possible. The remains of the wreck lay off Cape Gelidonya, on the southern coast of Turkey, not far from the port of Finike. Since the sponge divers had reported there were at least two different types of bronze tool there, it seemed highly likely that the cargo might date from the Bronze Age, and this was reinforced by their account of the degraded state of the metal, since Roman wrecks usually produced bronze in fairly good condition. A wreck cargo as early as the Bronze Age was quite unheard of in the Mediterranean at that time, so the site was obviously well worth investigating.

In the following summer Throckmorton managed to arrange a visit by an American diving expedition. For two days they followed

Captain Kemal's directions and searched the sea-bed, but found nothing. Then, on the last planned dive before their departure, quite by chance they saw a piece of heavily-overgrown bronze. Two lumps were broken off and brought to the surface. When cleaned, they turned out to be a bronze ploughshare and half a bronze double-axe, broken at the socket. Before bad weather forced them to leave, the expedition had sketched and photographed the wreck site and lifted further bronze tools and two bronze ingots. Subsequent examination confirmed that these dated from the late Bronze Age, around 1200 BC. The oldest shipwreck so far known had been found, and nautical archaeology was about to come of age.

The expedition which arrived off Cape Gelidonya the following year, in 1960, had Peter Throckmorton as technical adviser, Frederick Dumas, a veteran of many French underwater operations, as chief diver and Joan du Plat Taylor of the Institute of Archaeology in London as chief conservator. The man in charge was George Bass who, fresh from his YMCA training, made his first sea-dive with Throckmorton on one side of him and Dumas on the other. The expedition had its base on a rocky beach noted for its heat, flies and rock-falls from the cliffs above. Most of the conservation of objects and writing-up of records was done there, while the divers went out each day in one or two sponge boats to anchor near the wreck. The idea was to use an airlift, a type of suction hose. Air is pumped down to a hole near its bottom and then allowed to rise. This creates a suction effect at the mouth of the hose, which sucks up through the pipe to the surface any small loose object near it on the sea-bed. For recording, methods broadly evolved by Cousteau, Tailliez and the Italian, Lamboglia, were used. The latter in particular had pioneered the use of a grid, first of tape, then of steel, for recording the lay-out of wrecks and cargo on the bottom, and it was hoped to improve on these techniques. At first, in Throckmorton's own words, Bass drove the divers mad. He insisted on the same standard of recording, before any object was lifted, as was normal on a dry-land excavation. Soon, however, the divers came to accept that this was the way of the future. Though there were still shortcomings, by the end the dig itself, as well as its finds, had earned their places in history, and the story of the Cape Gelidonya wreck could be pieced together with remarkable precision.

Round about 1200 BC, towards the end of the Bronze Age in that part of the Mediterranean, a small trader some thirty-five feet (10·62 metres) long with a ton of cargo aboard was coasting westward off the southern shore of Turkey; but it failed to make the passage between the two large islands off Cape Gelidonya, an area described by the Roman writer, the Younger Pliny, as 'extremely dangerous to mariners'. After striking some jagged rocks, the hull of the ship ended up between the base of one of the islands and a large boulder some ninety feet down. There was no sand there to cushion or protect the timbers and by the time the excavators arrived, three thousand years later, almost every surviving thing was covered with a coralline concretion as hard as cement and up to eight inches thick. To add to the problems, the bottom was too irregular to use the plotting frame, so recording had to be done laboriously by triangulation, that is by measuring a series of triangles from a base line and by knowing the length of the sides of the triangles and the angles, mapping any given position. The positions of different objects were marked on sheets of frosted plastic taken down by the divers, and a photographic montage of the site was put together.

It would have been impossible to excavate each object individually, so it was decided to raise the concretion in massive lumps after recording. These were then re-assembled like a jig-saw on dry land and excavated, their relevant positions once more being recorded. A few careful taps with a hammer and sometimes the concretion would fall away cleanly from the metal object inside. Other pieces needed chisels or a vibrating electric point to clean them.

The first large lump of concretion on the sea-bed refused to move at all. Only by using a hydraulic jack from the expedition's jeep was the three-hundred-pound mass eventually freed from the bottom. They then had to sway it up to the sponge boat on the surface above by winch. Though this method worked, there was a risk all the time, if the boat happened to roll at the wrong moment, of damaging either boat or divers, so they changed to another way which has become standard in most underwater excavations since then. A deflated cloth balloon was lashed to the piece of concretion to be lifted. The balloon was then filled with air from a pipe or aqualung and up the piece floated. Weights of up to four hundred pounds could be handled in this way.

So they proceeded until the work was done. In Throckmorton's view, the excavation was a reasonable technical success, and they recovered about ninety-five per cent of the material visible from the wreck. For Bass, the results were both spectacular and of

OPPOSITE
George Bass holds a ranging pole on a mark while another member of the team records the measurement taken from the pole.

Some of the thirty-four copper ingots still stacked on the seabed as they were in the hold of the Cape Gelidonya ship in the late Bronze Age.

great historical importance. From this one excavation emerged a more detailed picture of the contents of a Bronze Age ship, and how and why it had traded than had ever been available before.

The cargo consisted mainly of four-handled ingots of copper and 'bun' ingots of bronze, all carefully packed in mat baskets, as well as a considerable quantity of broken or unfinished tools. The different nature of these is a reflection of the technology of the Bronze Age: hoes, picks, axes, adzes, a shovel, chisels, knives, bowls, pins, spearheads like the one Captain Kemal had first found, and a spit for roasting meat. There was also some casting waste and some bits of broken ingot. This collection was by far the largest hoard of metal implements of pre-Classical times ever found. What was more, it did not just indicate the cargo of the sunken ship: by carefully recording the position of everything found, it was possible to tell what had been cargo and what had been the personal possessions of the people on board.

Among the latter were a pair of very smooth stone mace-heads of the sort that were used for hammering bronze. There were also some polishers and whetstones and three large flattish stones of the type used as anvils in the days before iron was available. So there had evidently been a tinker on board. To him also would have belonged the set of balance-pan weights, which were necessary for calculating the price of scrap metal. These weights were particularly interesting for two reasons. They could be made up into different sets, which would have enabled the tinker to trade in many different countries—Egypt, Syria, Palestine, Cyprus, Troy, the Hittite Empire, Crete and possibly even the Greek mainland. They were also more accurate than archaeologists had previously believed possible of this period.

Other personal possessions also proved important because, in contrast to the cargo which clearly came from Cyprus, these belongings came from Syria. The cylinder seal, an essential then for any merchant to mark his goods, was Syrian, as was the only oil-lamp found. Altogether the finds suggested to Bass a Syrian scrap-metal dealer, who was also a tinker, making his way from Cyprus by the coast of Turkey to the Aegean, supplementing his rations with olives and fish, perhaps playing knuckle-bones in his spare moments by the light of the single lamp. It is a picture at once detailed and intimate, and the pottery and radio-carbon dates from the scraps of wood in the wreck coincide in telling us that it ended on the rocks off Cape Gelidonya somewhere about 1200 BC.

There was nothing grand about this craft or its crew. It was essentially a tramp or small merchantman. Yet it has caused the re-writing of a good deal of history. One ship alone does not necessarily make a fleet, but the excavation of the Gelidonya wreck inspired a series of studies which have shown that this one vessel does in fact represent a general trend. Previously, widespread finds of Mycenaean pottery of this period had suggested that sailors from the mainland of Greece dominated sea trade at this time. Now we know that Phoenicians from Syria played an important part in it as well. They took metal westward, and possibly cloth and ivory, just as the Cape Gelidonya ship was doing, but left very little pottery behind them as evidence to suggest this activity. On the way back from Mycenae in return they took wine, honey, olives, pickled fish, all packed in Mycenaean pottery receptacles; and it is these pottery remains that gave archaeologists the entirely false impression that there was a Greek monopoly of this trade.

Furthermore, one of the reasons for giving a late date to the writing of Homer's *Odyssey* has been the frequent mention in it of the activity of Phoenician merchants. Now that we know this Phoenician trading was going on by the twelfth century BC, we may have to revise our ideas about when Homer lived and wrote. A few scraps from the sea-bed can influence literary history as well.

With all these additions to our knowledge, there was one thing this excavation did not do. It did not reveal what a Bronze Age ship was like in itself. Only odd bits of wood from the hull survived where they had lain sheltered by pieces of cargo. For what it may have looked like we still have to rely on the sort of material that was available to Bass's predecessors—engravings, models, paintings on vases. Perhaps the best of these, for this particular purpose, is a terracotta model from Byblos dating from a little before 1200 BC. This has a rounded shape, with matching bow and stern and a raised platform at each end protected by a high palisade. The model has projections at each end, which were used to hang it up in a temple as an offering for a successful voyage, but it has also been suggested that they were copied from the actual hull as well and represent real projections at bow and stern. In that case the vessel, unlike early Egyptian ones, must have had a keel, as it is highly unlikely that the projections would have been there without a keel to spring from. The ships of the 'Sea Peoples', shown on the battle scene on the Temple of Medinet-Habu in Egypt, are both different from the Egyptian craft and to some extent similar to the Byblos model. They too have a high matching bow and stern with a protected platform. One craft even has a small projection at its bow; its very smallness may reflect the Egyptian sculptor's unfamiliarity with this strange piece of naval architecture.

These examples show some of the problems that exist when trying to visualise ancient ships in this sort of way where there is a shortage of evidence. Actual remains are a very different matter; and it was not long after 1960 that a good deal more than was left of the Cape Gelidonya wreck began to appear in the Mediterranean, and, for the first time, to be properly recorded.

The terracotta model from Byblos of a Phoenician merchantman.

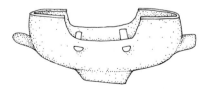

3

Classical Ships: the Sea-bed Robbers

In late 1969 police at Reggio di Calabria arrested a group of divers who had been looting a shipwreck in the Straits of Messina off Sicily and selling their finds in Italy and abroad. Subsequently the leader of the group was sentenced to five years' imprisonment for his 'crime against the state'. Not many underwater excavations have started because of a criminal prosecution, but this was so in the case of the Porticello ship, as it was called. For after the illegal divers had drawn attention to the richness of the finds from this wreck, the Italian Department of Antiquities invited the University Museum of Pennsylvania to see what they could rescue in a properly conducted excavation. This was duly organised by David Owen, a former member of George Bass's team.

The nature of the site also made it rather different from most other underwater excavations. The swift currents of the Straits of Messina meant it was essential to use only experienced divers; this, combined with the dense water traffic, made it impossible to anchor a barge or other vessel over the site. Instead, marker buoys were laid near the wreck. The divers then rode out to them in inflatable boats and having secured the boats to the buoys, dived down to the wreck holding on to the line from the buoy. With the currents running at five knots this was important, because it would have been very easy to be swept away.

Their first job was to make a metal-detector survey of the area of the wreck, whose general whereabouts was well known locally. With white string and wooden posts, lanes one metre wide were put down, and along these the three-man US Navy team, who, together with six members of the University Museum of Pennsyl-

27

vania and five Italian *carabinieri*, made up the divers of the team, worked their way with their metal detector. Each contact they found was marked with a wooden stake, thus avoiding any interference with the sensitivity of their machine. These contacts were then excavated either by hand or by an airlift which with some difficulty was brought to the site. As most people who have used metal-detecting machines know only too well, many of the contacts turned out to be modern in origin. Tins, bits of wire rope, anchors, bottle tops, even nailed shoes were found. All the same, in this case there were also finds of antique lead, copper, bronze, silver and iron.

When the survey had been completed, four areas stood out in importance and these were excavated down to bedrock. The loose sand on top was never more than twenty inches (fifty centimetres) deep, so it was possible to clear them quickly. This was lucky because the current soon refilled excavated areas, anything light that was disturbed, like bits of wood, was quickly swept away, and the divers were only allowed twenty-minute sessions at the 124-foot (37-metre) depth of the wreck. The positions of all objects were recorded by triangulation from fixed points each side of the wreck, and this information was put down on plastic sheets carried by the divers. Only large objects were given the honour of being photographed where they lay.

As with the Cape Gelidonya ship, the distribution of the finds soon revealed where the cabin had been. From this area came a wooden bowl, black glazed cups and pieces of cooking pots. A wooden fishing-line reel and lead sinkers told of one way the crew whiled away their time in supplementing their shipboard rations. The rarest find was an iron-tipped wooden-handled sailmaker's awl, the earliest evidence for sail-mending so far found, since the objects pointed to a late fifth-century BC date for the ship's sinking.

The cargo had consisted of rather more than two hundred amphorae, of which only twelve had escaped the looters' attention and remained on the sea bed for the excavators to record properly before lifting. They were of eight types, and were Greek or Carthaginian in origin. Among those recovered by the police from two hundred or so that had been looted were some that were still full of the pitch which had been used to line all of them to stop leaking and sweating.

Moving up the ship from the cabin past the cargo, the divers found the bow area had also suffered from the looters. It was known that a huge one-thousand-kilo lead anchor-stock had come from this area, before being cut up by the looters and sold for scrap. Two smaller lead stocks from here, with Greek or Phoenician inscriptions to add to their interest, had met the same fate. All that was left for the excavators were four lead bars, which had been part of the anchor's construction, and two pointed bronze tips which had protected the wooden flukes of one of the anchors. A third one of these bronze tips, which was recovered by the police, was added evidence for the use of more than one anchor on these ships. Though in the end the excavators acquired enough information to reconstruct the detail of an anchor of the fifth century BC, the loss of the other actual parts was still a pity.

Ancient anchors have proved a very worthwhile study. Triangular stones with holes in them lying in various Mediterranean temples were once thought to be mysterious cult objects. Now they are known to be something much more practical—anchors. Classical literature confirms the practice of leaving anchors in temples as offerings. One example is that of the Milesians who traditionally are said to have found Hercules' anchor at the fountain of Astacis where the Argonauts had left it, and brought it home as an offering for their temple of Athena Jasonica.

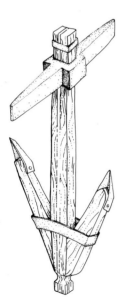

A reconstruction of a composite Roman anchor with its lead stock and collar.

The efficiency of stone anchors was improved by putting pointed sticks through holes in them, and this led in turn to bent-up sticks and eventually to the true anchors, as we would know them, of the Greeks and Romans. According to the historian Strabo, a Greek called Anarcharsis who lived about 500 BC was responsible for inventing the anchor with arms, and this is to some extent confirmed by the finding of a lead stock on a sixth-century BC wreck off the coast of Antibes in France. Because these anchors were attached to ropes, not chains, they came easily off the sea-bed unless they were weighted somehow. Hence the lead stocks, which kept the flukes biting into the bottom and survived when the wooden parts of the anchor had long since rotted away. Because the lead had scrap value, such ancient anchor-stocks had long since vanished from the eastern Mediterranean, where sponge divers collected any that were visible. More survived in the western Mediterranean because there was no major sponge industry there, but this situation is rapidly being changed by amateur divers, though now the curiosity or souvenir value of the anchor-stocks to tourists is overtaking what they fetch as scrap. Peter Throckmorton knew one man who claimed he had lifted thirty tons of ancient lead anchor-stocks in just one twenty-mile stretch of coast!

Like that of the Porticello ship itself, this story illustrates the damage the aqualung has done to the material of history on the sea-bed, as well as the advantages it has brought by making proper scientific excavation possible. All over the world the looting of underwater sites is a problem, from Norway to Western Australia. Dynamite is often the looter's chief weapon, as it was with a first-century BC Roman wreck at Dramont. Surviving pieces of amphora tell us it was bringing wine from Campagna in Italy to Narbonne in France, but since it was blown up by skin divers in 1957 no one will ever know what sort of ship it was. Even sadder was the case of one of the large number of wrecks looted in the fifties in French waters. It was an Etruscan one of the sixth century BC. Etruscan ships are a subject of some interest because a tomb painting of the fourth century BC from Tarquinia in Italy shows one of the earliest known pictures of a two-masted sailing ship, and there is no known actual example of this shipbuilding tradition. An Etruscan wreck would therefore have been of great interest and justified very considerable efforts at recovery, but this one off Nice was completely robbed and lost before any archaeologist even knew of its existence.

The Mediterranean is notorious because of its many classical wrecks, clear water, sunshine, and good diving conditions. But Britain is unique in another way. Even if they cannot always enforce the laws and police the sea-bed properly, other countries have at least passed laws to protect their antiquities underwater. Although the British have protected ancient monuments on land since 1880 and are a maritime country, it was not until 1973 that they passed a law to protect anything below the high-water mark. Hence the extraordinary happenings which marked the finding of King Charles II's yacht, the *Mary*, off Anglesey in 1971; there were rumours of looted cannon being hidden in coffins, shotguns fired over the heads of rival motorboats, lead weights dropped on divers' bubbles—all more like the ingredients of a fictional thriller than what should have been a serious archaeological study.

Unfortunately it is normal throughout most of the world for treasure-hunting efforts far to outnumber proper excavations. In Throckmorton's view, it is probably safe to say that there are no visible wrecks left in French, Spanish or Italian waters in less than 150 feet (47·75 metres) of water which have not been pretty well looted and destroyed.

The Porticello ship was therefore a worthwhile exception, even though most of its wooden hull now consisted of either

A reconstruction of a two-masted Etruscan ship from a tomb painting at Tarquinia.

The salvaged remains of one of the Nemi ships in the lakeside museum before it was destroyed during the last war.

shapeless fragments or the skeletons of wood-worms. Still, enough did remain to show that its strakes had been fastened to each other by mortices and tenons, that copper nails had been used in its construction, and that it had lead sheathing. This confirmed the evidence from two ships which were so unusual that many people once thought they could not be typical. These were the two great Roman vessels from Lake Nemi in Italy which are believed to have been the Emperor Caligula's pleasure barges. In themselves these vast craft, over 230 feet (70 metres) long, have experienced almost the whole history of early diving. Their presence on the bottom of Lake Nemi had never been forgotten when, in the fifteenth century AD, the architect Leon Battista Alberti first sent Genoese swimmers down to explore them. He then tried to raise the craft by hooks on the ends of ropes led up to a raft of barrels. Less than a century later, Francesco Demarchi, wearing a wooden helmet with a small crystal plate to see through, made what may well have been the earliest use of a diving suit. Then in the nineteenth century a diving bell was lowered on to the wrecks. All these various methods revealed that the ships had brick pavings, metal columns, mosaics,

OPPOSITE
Above Building an
Egyptian boat in the
early part of the third
millennium BC.
The rope over the
forked stick is being
taughtened by twisting
it with a rod, and two
props under the bow
and stern are also
helping to keep the
correct shape of the
vessel.
Below An Egyptian
sailing ship from the
same date. The two-
legged mast and the
many backstays are
survivals of the time
when the hull was
built of papyrus. Both
reliefs come from the
tomb of the courtier
Nefer at Saqqara.

marble statues and many other wonders. Finally, in the nineteen thirties, Mussolini had the lake drained and the huge barges saw the light of day for the first time for nearly two thousand years and were put on display in a museum.

But there was not to be a happy ending to the story. On the 31st May 1944, the Allied attack on Rome was at its height. A German anti-aircraft battery near the museum which housed the great vessels had been in action all day. That night, at about ten o'clock, smoke and flames started bursting out of the windows of the museum, and not long afterwards the building and its contents were totally ablaze. Whether shells which had struck the building earlier in the day had set it alight, or whether it was done through wanton spite by soldiers from the battery no one knows for certain. The ships had at least established that Roman vessels were built 'shell fashion': that is to say, the main strength came from the covering of the hull, the planks of which were joined to each other by tongues of wood fitting into the thickness of each adjoining pair of planks and secured by wooden dowels passing through plank and tongue alike. Inside this shell were then put frames (the lateral timbers, attached to the planks, which gave a ship its shape) very close together. The whole thing was done so neatly and securely that it was more like cabinet-makers' than what we would call shipwrights' work. As far as we know, this technique was pretty well universal throughout the Graeco-Roman world and lasted many centuries. It contrasts with the 'skeleton' method in which the keel is laid down, the bow and stern pieces and ribs added and finally planks attached to cover up the 'skeleton'.

In the Nemi ships, even though they must have spent their entire existence in fresh water, the underwater part of the hull was sheathed with lead fastened on by copper nails. In salt water this protected ships from the burrowing of the teredo worm.

The burning of the Nemi ships left at that time only one truly classical ship actually in existence on dry land, and only part of one at that. This was the remains of a small cargo vessel, probably of the second century AD, found during a building excavation in 1864 at Marseilles and optimistically, and quite inaccurately, christened 'Caesar's Galley'. But in 1965 a chain of events began in Cyprus which was to give nautical archaeologists a much richer source of information about the work of Graeco-Roman shipwrights.

4

The Kyrenia Ship: Nine Thousand Salted Almonds

Andreas Cariolou is a sponge-diver from the town of Kyrenia in Cyprus. He works single-handed and is in many ways a remarkable man. One day in 1965 he anchored his boat in a familiar place over a deep reef where he had often before collected sponges. The difference on this particular day was that while he was down on the reef picking the sponges and putting them in his bag, he noticed the anchor of his boat starting to drag away from the reef into deeper water. He at once followed it, for otherwise he would have to surface far from his boat and have a long swim to it with his sponges. He used the wisps of mud the anchor threw up as it bumped along the sea-bed as a guide, and it was while he was doing this that something caught the corner of his eye. It was a pile of amphorae, neatly stacked in rows as though still on the deck of an ancient merchant-man. Intrigued by this unfamiliar sight, he stayed over the wreck as long as his air-supply lasted. When he came to the surface, he found himself in a near gale which had by now carried his boat half a mile away. In the course of regaining his boat, he understandably did not take bearings to identify the spot where he had found the amphorae. It was to be two years before he found them again.

By that time a diving team from the University Museum of Pennsylvania had arrived in Cyprus to search for wrecks, led by Michael Katzev and his wife Susan, who had met each other during George Bass's excavation of the Yassi Ada ship (see Chapter 5). They heard rumours of a diver who knew of some sunken pottery. Fortunately for posterity, Cariolou was not a man searching for a quick profit from treasure-hunting. He had an interest in the antiquity of his country and a deep concern for the future of his

An underwater archaeologist working with an airlift on the sea bed at the site of the Porticello ship.

33

community. He kept resolutely quiet about the location of the wreck until such time as it looked as though it could be properly excavated and the finds kept together in the town of Kyrenia. The arrival of the Pennsylvania expedition gave him his cue, and soon he was manoeuvring a boat with the Americans aboard over the site of the wreck.

When they saw for themselves what Cariolou had seen, the American divers were a little puzzled. The cargo of close-packed amphorae covered an area of only sixteen by ten feet (4·88 by three metres). Could the vessel be just a tender, or was it some exceptionally small cargo craft?

To settle the problem, the expedition called on two pieces of equipment from the Oxford University Research Laboratory for Archaeology and the History of Art—a proton magnetometer designed by Dr E. Hall and a metal detector designed by Jeremy Green, both well-known figures in the world of underwater technology. The two instruments work on different principles. The proton magnetometer is passive; it does not send out any signal of its own, it merely records differences in the earth's magnetic field. If it moves over a collection of cannon on the sea-bed, for instance, it gives a different reading from when it is over sand. The metal detector, on the other hand, transmits a radio signal which is reflected back differently from such different targets as metal and rocks.

The expedition first laid down a cord grid of six and a half feet (two-metre) squares. Then they worked over it with the magnetometer. This revealed two concentrations of metal outside the area of the amphorae. The metal detector picked them up, too, and a number of other contacts as well. When all these were plotted on a plan, the expedition realised that the wreck was indeed larger than its visible cargo suggested. This was confirmed when they probed the areas of the contacts with a thin metal rod. They now found that the pile of amphorae was much larger than it had first seemed but that much of it was covered by sand and weed. The whole stack in fact stretched for some sixty-three by thirty-three feet (nineteen by ten metres). What was more, the axis of this area was different from that suggested by the visible amphorae. Most important of all, perhaps, the bottom appeared to be muddy sand; they therefore had a large cargo ship with its load apparently still in position, and a good chance of much of the wood of the hull under the cargo being preserved in the sand of the sea-bed. Everything was set for a highly promising season of excavation the following year.

The cargo of amphorae which first drew attention to the presence of the Kyrenia ship.

The first thing the excavators had to do in the 1968 season was to remove the heavy layer of sand which covered, as they now knew, most of the ship's cargo. This was made more difficult by a thick matting of eel-grass roots in the sand layer. They got rid of this by undermining the whole layer with a water-jet, then bubbling compressed air from a needle probe round the roots to loosen them from the sand which held them. The matting of grass could then be cut and pulled away in sections. In this way the precise extent of the cargo was eventually revealed. The eighty or so amphorae which Cariolou had originally seen became in the end more than four hundred. These were of ten different shapes in all; the vast majority, which were for wine, came from the island of Rhodes, and dated from the last part of the fourth century BC. Many were empty, but to the surprise of the excavators several were found to hold almonds still preserved in their shells. Masses of these nuts were also found loose in the hull—more than nine thousand shells were recovered. It was thought more likely they had once been in sacks which had rotted, rather than that they had been used to help the cargo

35

stowage, like the eight hundred tons of lentils which Pliny reported had been taken as ballast in the huge vessel of perhaps 1,400 tons which the Emperor Caligula used to bring an obelisk from Alexandria to stand on the Vatican hill in Rome in the first century AD. It is probable that the almonds had come from Cyprus, which was famous for its almonds in antiquity.

The cargo had yet another surprise for the excavators—a large number of stone grain-mills. A grain-mill consisted of an upper and a lower part. Grain would be fed into a slot in the top, and as the mill was rotated to and fro by a bar across the top part, the grain would be ground between the corrugated surfaces of the two stones. Twenty-nine of these blocks were found; but when they were ballooned to the surface in wire baskets, they posed an intriguing problem: although they had mason's marks consisting of single Greek letters chiselled into their sides, they did not pair up. In fact there was an extraordinary disparity of size, shape and finish. The suggested solution was that they must have been the spoiled remnants of an earlier cargo which had been kept on board for ballast.

As with the Cape Gelidonya and Porticello ships, the cabin areas fore and aft were distinguishable by their contents. Pottery plates, bowls, ladles, sieves and a copper cauldron were part of the eating equipment of the crew. Four drinking cups, four salt dishes, four oil jugs and four wooden spoons strongly hinted at the number of the ship's complement. As with the Porticello ship, there were lead weights for fishing and a single oil lamp. This seemed to confirm the tradition that the Greeks of that time only sailed by daylight if they possibly could, while later Roman fleets sailed by night as well as day. Roman ships carried lights to keep in company at night, and the average speeds of four and a half to six knots of some voyages reported in the classical authors could have been achieved only by day and night sailing.

Perhaps the most unusual find on the Kyrenia ship was an inkwell. The owner must have needed written records to keep track of the wine, olives and pickled fish in all those different amphorae!

At the end of the 1968 season the site was covered with plastic sheets and sand to protect it during the winter, and the excavation was resumed the following summer. As the 1969 season drew to a close, a difficult decision faced Katzev: should he cover the site up again for another winter, or try to salvage the ship itself without delay? By now all the cargo had been lifted, and it was clear that

OPPOSITE
Under the measuring frames the stone grain-mills which seem to have been used as ballast for the Kyrenia ship lie on the bottom timbers.

their original hopes about the hull had been more than confirmed: the ship was fifty-two feet (15·8 metres) long, and about fifty per cent of the wood was preserved, divided into the two halves into which the hull had split, just to starboard of the keel line, some time during its 2,000 years on the sea bed. But already the divers had observed a noticeable softening of those timbers which they had uncovered first, and it seemed certain this process would continue, however carefully they tried to protect the wood over the next winter. Besides, the outer planks had already been riddled by teredo worms in antiquity, and a fresh attack would almost certainly finish them off. Finally, there was the risk that treasure-hunters or souvenir-seekers might loot or damage this immensely important wreck, for its location had by now been well established by the expedition's diving operations. So, in spite of all the problems that would be involved, Katzev decided to lift. It was a bold decision to raise a whole wreck which had lain ninety feet (27·4 metres) down on the sea-bed for 2,000 years.

One of the first difficulties had nothing to do with the sea: it was how to get the remains of the wreck over the eighty-foot (24·4-metre) wall of Kyrenia's Crusader Castle into the courtyard where its preservation and reconstruction were going to take place. There was no crane on the island that could do the job. A helicopter was rejected because of the effect of the down draught of the rotors on the softened wood. At one time the Cyprus Department of Antiquities even offered to knock down the castle wall, but the expedition declined this with thanks. In the end Katzev decided the only practical course was to cut the wreck up on the sea-bed into pieces small enough to go through the castle doorway.

The excavators started on the smaller, eastern side of the ship. Using a compressed-air underwater saw, they cut out pieces approximately one metre by two in size. Under each of these was slid a flexible sheet of galvanised iron, which in its turn was moved onto a rigid metal frame with flexible supports to take the curved pieces. This frame was then taken to the surface by inflated balloons with a diver accompanying it, spilling air as necessary from the balloons so that it did not come up too swiftly. On the surface, the frame was winched onto a waiting boat and taken ashore to a lorry which very slowly and carefully drove into the castle court, where the wood was placed in fresh-water tanks. But in spite of every care, it was found that with this method they were up against one of the constant difficulties of sea-bed excavation—the softness of wood which has lain under water for any length of time. One of Peter Throckmorton's classic underwater stories is about a gastronomically-minded Belgian at a dinner party who was having explained to him the problem of raising wood from the sea-bed when it had become as soft as cheese. 'What exact sort of cheese?' he asked. 'Not too ripe camembert,' was the reply

Timbers of this consistency, however carefully they were handled, tended to lose their original shape between the sea-bed and the castle courtyard. It soon became clear that each section of the ship would have to be dismantled and restored to its original shape after preservation and before any reconstruction could begin. So for the western side of the ship it was decided not to saw it into sections but to dismantle it on the sea-bed and lift it piece by piece. First the ribs were taken up and laid on their sides on the lifting tray. Then the mast-step complex was removed and the keel, after it had been cut into manageable lengths. Last of all were the outer planks. In the castle the pieces were washed clean of any mud sticking to them and the shape of the ribs traced before being put into fresh water for the first stage of conservation.

Long before any dismantling happened, a full record was made of the shape of the ship on the sea-bed. As each part was uncovered, it was recorded by a stereo-plotter lent by Karlsruhe University, which worked to an accuracy of two centimetres. When Joachim Hohle, the German photogrammetrist, had to leave at the end of August, the remaining parts were recorded by a system of pointing rods. This manually-operated device measured the position of each piece of hull in both depth and plan with a similar sort of accuracy.

The information from these two devices was vital for Laina Wylde, the attractive blonde architect who was going to try and work out the original shape of the ship for its reconstruction. One thing was clear. The ship, like the Nemi and Porticello ones, was built shell-first. The planks had been fastened to each other by mortices made in the thickness of the strakes into which tenons had been driven. The planks were of pine, perhaps because pine grew on Cyprus and seems to have been better than the local fir; fir, though, was preferred for faster, more manoeuvrable warships because it was lighter.

One can imagine the care with which the planks were chosen, since they had to take all this elaborate joinery. If the wood was too dry, it might split. If it was too green, it might shrink as it dried, and leave the tenons too much play. Possibly the tenons

A ship with Odysseus tied to the mast. From a Greek vase of the fifth-century BC.

39

may even have been greased, so they could be knocked home to make a really tight fit. One result of this method was that Roman ships rarely had any caulking, and the historian Strabo was surprised at the Venetii tribe on the Bay of Biscay who used seaweed to caulk their ships, which were probably built in a quite different tradition.

Next the ribs were laid inside on top of the planks and fixed in position by copper nails driven in from outside the hull and clenched over the inside face of the ribs. An interesting point about the ribs was that they were of different sizes. One sort spanned the keel and then had extension pieces which presumably ran up to the gunwhale. The next only ran from just short of the keel to above the turn of the bilge. On these ribs were laid the ceiling planks or flooring timbers, on which the cargo was stowed. These had Greek letter-symbols carved into their surfaces, which, like those on the Cheops ship, may have been keying signs to show where each fitted. Like the Porticello and Nemi ships, the outside of the hull was sheathed with lead fastened by rows of copper tacks. The excavators even found extra rolls of lead sheeting and carpenters' mallets on board for emergency repairs. Often the lead was put on over a layer of wool, linen or tarred fabric. Finally the outside was covered with pitch, wax, or paint, or various combinations of these ingredients, so its colour could range from black all over to brighter blue, yellow, purple, brown or green, though often the brightest colours were used just for decoration.

One of the most fascinating aspects of these Mediterranean wrecks is the way they have cleared up arguments that have been going on for years about how certain passages in classical authors should be translated. For instance, Ovid describes in a dramatic passage in his *Metamorphoses* how the 'wedges' of a ship 'work loose, and the seam, stripped of its covering of wax, lies open and furnishes a path for the death-dealing waters.' '*Cunei*', the Latin word for wedges, was a puzzle, till the wrecks made it clear that Ovid was referring to the tenons which joined the planks: when they worked loose, the planks opened up, the wax outer cover parted and the water came pouring in.

In the same way, Homer's description of how Odysseus built a ship, in the course of which he 'hammered it with pegs and joints', was very puzzling until one could see it in terms of fitting planks together by knocking tenons into mortices. So divers are helping to rewrite Greek and Latin dictionaries.

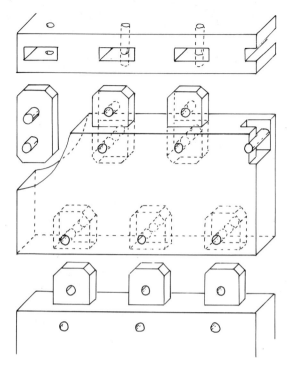

Mortice and tenon construction. Wooden tenons which fitted into the thickness of the adjoining planks were held in place by circular dowels driven through them.

A problem that neither excavation nor literature can solve at the moment is what the sail of the Kyrenia ship was like. The intricacy of the mast-step, in Katzev's words, was, in this lowly and common form of cargo ship, a tribute to the skill of the Greek shipwrights who built her. Another intriguing revelation of this same skill was that there seem to have been two positions for the mast. This is yet another case of a new find adding to our admiration for these ancient navigators.

In the stern area the excavators found more than a hundred lead rings. These are usually thought to have been sewn to the front of the sail to take the brails. These were ropes which ran up from the deck through the rings, over the yard and down to the deck again. By hauling on them, a small crew could very quickly and efficiently shorten sail in a squall. Because sails at this time often had ropes or strips of leather sewn horizontally across them for added strength, the brails, running at right angles, would account for the chequer-board appearance of sails in some classical illustrations.

So American, Cypriot, British and German skills and efforts have led to what should eventually be a remarkable sight—a fully reconstructed ship which is the earliest so far to be raised from the bottom of the sea. We cannot be sure what quirk of fate chose this ship, so unremarkable in its own day, to become so exceptional in ours. The coins which were found on board, of Antigonus 'the One-eyed' and Demetrius 'the Besieger', heirs to parts of Alexander the Great's empire, show that she could not have sunk earlier than 306 BC. Her cargo of almonds gave a radio-carbon date of 288 BC ± 62, which fitted well enough. Yet the wood from her hull yielded dates of 389 BC ± 44. So the Kyrenia ship was probably eighty years old when her career as a cargo tramp ended. Just why it ended when it did has to be a matter of guesswork. There are no shallow hidden reefs nearby, and there are no signs of piracy or fire. The absence of any personal possessions, on the other hand, except for the eyelets and leather of a sailor's sandal, suggests that the crew abandoned her.

Perhaps a sudden gale blew up, like the one that moved Cariolou's boat. They would have lowered the sail at once, and probably the mast too, and stowed them in the after part, which might explain the lead rings. Then they would have thrown out more anchors, including what the Greeks called the 'sacred anchor', the last or sheet anchor. Perhaps the cargo shifted and they reckoned she was done for. But at least the captain seems to have had time to gather up his personal possessions, since the excavators found no sign of them. We are fortunate now to have the ship to study; perhaps he was also fortunate and managed to reach the shore safely.

5

Yassi Ada:
Bedsteads and Bicycle
Spokes

The sea-bed has its accident black-spots just like any city or traffic system. The Eddystone Light near Plymouth, in Devon, marks one famous one. There is a place off the coast of Sicily near Syracuse where a Roman merchantman, a medieval vessel, a nine-teenth-century sailing ship and a modern tanker all lie together in common disaster on the sea-bed. The island of Yassi Ada off the south coast of Turkey some sixteen miles from the town of Bodrum is yet another. This small barren island is undistinguished except for two things that may possibly be connected—the vast number of rats there, and a reef which runs out from where, logically, it should not, sometimes as little as six feet (1·83 metres) below the surface of the sea. No one knows how many ships have come to grief there, but there are visible remains of more than a dozen. When Peter Throck-morton was first taken there by Captain Kemal Aras, he saw the unusual sight of Ottoman cannon balls lying on the reef in between Roman amphorae. A little way away were coloured glass ingots, some as large as a man's head, of unknown date. Altogether the remains varied in date from the third century BC to a sailing caique of the nineteen thirties. But perhaps the most interesting were two wrecks which had struck the reef and slipped off it, landing on a sandy patch to one side. As Peter Throckmorton rightly observed, this meant there was a good chance that some of their hulls might be preserved.

One was a wreck from the time of the Prophet Mahomet in the sixth century AD. The other, of a century or so later, appeared to be Byzantine, of the seventh century AD. Its visible remains consisted of a cargo of amphorae, several anchors, and an area of broken tiles

43

and cooking pots, which was at once identified as the galley. This wreck was to be the target for George Bass's next campaign after Cape Gelidonya.

The Cape Gelidonya expedition had provided invaluable experience and marked a new approach in nautical archaeology; but even so, Frederick Dumas, the veteran French diver, could still write afterwards that, 'No antique wreck has yet been examined and recorded in its entirety.' The four seasons of work on the Yassi Ada wreck, from 1961 to 1964, were to change all that. This was to be the classic excavation of a classic wreck, setting standards for all to follow, and which trained amongst others Susan and Michael Katzev and David Owen for their subsequent achievements at Kyrenia and Porticello.

The University Museum of Pennsylvania expedition to Yassi Ada was to be an altogether larger affair than that at Cape Gelidonya: there, seven people, three of whom had never dived before, had been equipped with pencils and plastic boards, tapes and surveyors' poles, three underwater cameras, two lifting balloons, a crowbar and an airlift. From local blacksmiths they had also acquired hammers, picks, chisels, a smaller airlift, a lifting basket, and there was also that hydraulic jack from the jeep. Now at Yassi Ada there were fifteen specialists, and, right from the beginning, instead of travelling out in a sponge boat to anchor off the site each day, they obtained for their much more complex equipment an old eighty-ton flat barge as a permanent working base over the site. This was secured to three points on the sea-bed so it could always be eased into the correct position overhead, whatever the currents were doing.

Even with their larger staff and fixed base, the depth at which the wreck lay, 120 feet (31 metres), meant that working time on the bottom was limited, so the story of the four years was one of ever-evolving means of quick and accurate recording and continually more efficient and productive use of available time.

To start with, they cleaned the cargo of its incrustation of weed with wire brushes. After this the frog-spawnlike pattern of amphorae, of which there were about nine hundred in all, was ready for recording. Every visible object was given a number on a plastic tag which was held permanently up towards any camera or artist by stiff wire stems. At first, simple triangulation with plane-tables was used to plot positions. Then the excavators moved on to the quicker technique of laying a number of wire grids over the wreck. Above these, artists with gridded sheets of plastic would hover and draw details of

The wire basket at the top of the airlift which caught objects sucked up with sand and mud. The bag below this was regularly taken up to the surface to be emptied and sifted.

whatever lay beneath them. The grids themselves were plotted for height, and distances taken from them to the various objects, but since the grids had not been put down level the resulting calculations became somewhat complicated.

When the top layer had been recorded and the first-ever accurate plan made of an amphora wreck, it was time to lift the massive clay jars themselves. About a hundred of the nine hundred available were brought to the surface for sampling, usually by turning them upside down and filling them with an air hose, to send them popping up to the surface. There was one risk about this which led to cautious handling; the amphorae had sometimes been used by moray eels as homes, and moray eels can inflict a nasty wound. The jars not sent to the surface were stacked neatly on the sea-bed away from the scene of the excavation.

45

This lifting process revealed a layer of sand over the wreck which was in its turn airlifted away. A large wire basket under a lifting balloon took any individual finds to the surface, but many others appeared by sifting carefully through the sand and shells brought up by the airlift. It was while this well-organised routine was going on that the expedition had its one and only near-disaster. Laurence Johne, one of the expedition's diving instructors, suddenly became a victim of the 'bends'.

This is the paralysis caused by bubbles produced in the blood through too quick a reduction of pressure as the diver comes to the surface. In the nineteenth century, when the general use of helmeted diving gear first became widespread, the 'bends' were attributed to colds or even rheumatism. The principle of nitrogen gas being absorbed into human tissue under pressure was correctly described by a French physiologist called Paul Bert as early as 1878. But, as Peter Throckmorton has said, Greek sponge divers were as likely to have heard of this research as they were to know the Lapland recipe for reindeer stew. Instead, they worked out their own rule-of-thumb methods, and their own cures too, such as putting a split-open dead chicken on the chest of the victim. From 1906 on, the world's navies started the more efficacious practice of making tables with lists of permitted times at different depths and the various stops that had to be made on the way up to allow the nitrogen under pressure in the blood to dissipate without forming bubbles. They also evolved pressure tanks which could treat divers with the 'bends' by recreating the pressure of deep water and then gradually reducing it.

It was the United States Navy's tables that Bass used, plus an additional margin for safety. Decompression could be a boring process. Hanging around for twenty minutes a few feet below the surface after a working dive was irksome. Nevertheless Bass insisted on exact observation of the rules, all dives were carefully timed, and the divers had to find their own ways of easing the boredom of decompression. A plastic board lowered on a string from the barge could be used to exchange notes with the surface. A paperback book was even fastened to one of the decompression stops on the wire, just as it was, and survived in a readable state for some time.

But in spite of all these precautions Laurence Johne came to the surface paralysed from the waist down. Just because of his insistence on safety margins, Bass did not have an adequate decompression chamber on hand to treat such a case. Eight hours in a small collapsible chamber at Bodrum did not produce a cure. But meanwhile a US Army light plane had been organised by the American Consul to take the patient to the large US Navy chamber at Istanbul. Its flight path was carefully routed to follow the coast at sea level because flying over any high ground in an unpressurised plane would have made the patient's condition even worse. Thirty-eight hours in the big chamber eventually achieved the cure, except for weakness in one leg. Fortunately this unexplained setback was the only one to affect the expedition in four years and more than six thousand working dives.

The plotting of the position of the cargo, anchors and galley was now succeeded by a new task, the recording of the actual hull itself. It was at this stage that George Bass thought of his 'bedsteads'. Nine angle-iron frames on legs were set up on the slope of the sea-bed in a series of steps. These were carefully levelled, and flat metal plates on their feet stopped them sinking into the sea-bed and altering the levels. On successive sections of these squares was mounted a tower which had a criss-cross grid of tightly-stretched cords at its base and fixed position for a camera at its apex. Since the water was very clear, a photographic record of each section was soon made. No camera skill was required. The instrument was simply put in position, the photograph taken, and the tower moved to the next section.

The problems came from the various distortions. For instance, only objects in the centre of a section were seen in true relation to the grid, so once again the expedition's architect had to correct his figures before applying all of them to the master plan.

Another problem was solved by practical rather than mathematical means. This was that, now the hull was uncovered, the slightest movement of the current or by a nearby diver tended to loosen bits of wood, which then floated away to be lost for ever. The ingenious answer was to raid the local bicycle industry, buy two thousand spokes, sharpen the ends, and stick them through every piece of wood, however small. In this way the whole wreck was literally spiked to the sea-bed until it had been fully recorded. The hull also survived a winter covered by rubberised cloth weighted down by stones. Possibly in other countries it would not have been left alone so conscientiously as it was by the many Turkish sponge divers who came to have a look at this strange new feature on the sea-bed.

Throughout the excavation every means possible had been used to increase the productivity of the work. There was now a rat-proof camp on Yassi Ada island itself, to save the daily boat trip from Bodrum, and the architect had only a short distance to go to dive down to the wreck and then return to his drawing board. Nevertheless a vast proportion of diving time was still spent just on recording. Bass's mind now turned to the idea of stereo-photography. After a good deal of discussion, a system was evolved in which a special camera moved along a level bar over the site, taking overlapping photographs, just like a reconnaissance aircraft in wartime mapping a stretch of the enemy countryside. Rather to everyone's surprise, the system worked. The 'bedsteads' had had their day. A machine enabled its operator on Yassi Ada island to transfer the information from the 'stereo pairs' of photographs on to the master plan.

This obsession with recording every scrap of detail might seem exaggerated. But the old truth holds—excavation is destruction, on the sea-bed as much as anywhere else. Only by recording every possible piece of information can it be justified. No one can possibly know during an excavation what information may eventually be needed from any given situation.

At Yassi Ada the recorded information certainly paid off as far as recreating the appearance of the wrecked ship was concerned. This work was in the hands of Frederick van Doorninck, Jr, of the University of California. The actual excavators found it hard to believe that from the soggy twisted scraps of wood they had brought up and the photographs of the wreck on the bottom it would ever be possible to arrive at a true picture of the craft as it originally was. But van Doorninck was able to do this because he had, in his own words, an accurate-state plan of every surviving scrap of wood of a size of any consequence found within the area, complete with every nail hole, bolt hole, score line, mortice, or any other significant feature.

From these he was able to calculate the position and original angle of every nail and bolt hole, and therefore the angle at which they were originally attached. The ship that emerged on his drawing board had started off with a keel of cypress wood some forty feet (12 metres) long. To this had been attached a stern-piece and, presumably, a similar bow-piece, though this part of the wreck had disappeared. Then the builders had added pine planks to each side, secured to each other in the classical fashion by tenons let into the thickness of the adjoining planks. But when the waterline was

OPPOSITE
Bowls, ladles, jugs and cups from the Kyrenia ship. They helped to date the merchantman to somewhere about 300 BC.

48

© 1968 BY NATIONAL GEOGRAPHIC SOCIETY

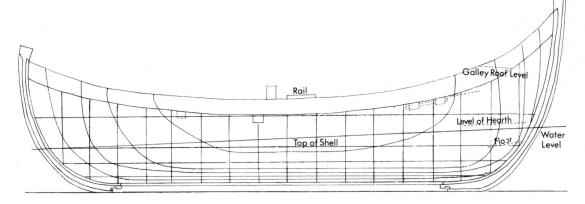

A preliminary impression of the lines of the seventh-century AD Yassi Ada ship. Much work and study has still to be done before the final version can be completed.

reached, there was a change of technique which was extremely significant. For this vessel, whose sinking was dated by the coins found in the wreck to AD 625 or 626, had been built at a cross-roads in shipbuilding methods. When the waterline level was reached the builders marked where the elm-wood ribs should go and then attached them by iron nails driven through the planks. From this stage onwards the builders were treating the vessel as a 'skeleton'. To the ribs which stood up high above the waterline they nailed or bolted heavy side-by-side pairs of planks and filled the gaps in between these heavy pairs with single nailed planks. And as in standard 'skeleton' construction, these planks were not fastened to each other by the hitherto familar tenons.

Next, deck beams were inserted across the width of the ship, supported at each end by L-shaped knees and possibly by posts as well. Two of the deck beams projected through each side of the hull to make an attachment point for the steering oars. Possibly two hatches, the mast, and the tiled roof of the galley would also have been fitted into the deck.

This chance find at Yassi Ada is extremely important to nautical archaeologists because it shows a transition stage from the classical 'shell' technique to an approach to the later 'skeleton' method. Another wreck nearby at Yassi Ada, which was later studied by Bass and could be dated to the fourth century AD, revealed an even earlier stage of this transition. Here the tenons attached the planks to each other all the way up to the gunwhale, but they had already become seven inches apart, more widespread therefore than the usual Roman practice, and by the time of the seventh-century Yassi Ada ship the tenons were as much as three feet apart.

Reconstruction painting by Pierre Mion of work in progress on the Yassi Ada wreck. Recording frames, cameras, airlift and lifting balloons are shown in use under the barge which was the divers' base.

No one knows exactly why there should have been this change of technique. George Bass suspects one reason may have been

49

D

Frederick van Doorninck Jnr. piecing together some of the fragments of the planking of the Yassi Ada ship.

that after the fall of the Roman Empire there was a reduction in the number of skilled shipwrights available to carry out this extremely detailed and time-consuming method of ship construction. The Belgian archaeologist, Lucien Basch, suggests that the process may have begun even earlier, when the Romans suddenly found themselves needing to take to the sea and build ships in large numbers. Some of their claimed achievements are quite remarkable. According to the classical author, Polybius, in 260 BC Rome built a fleet of a hundred quinquiremes and triremes in sixty days. Six years later she built 220 ships in three months. The 'shell' method of construction is very much dependent on the eye of the master shipwright. Basch suggests that the use of a mould or moulds to dictate a standard shape to the growing shell of planks would have made fast mass production much easier, and such moulds are well on the way to the idea of pre-erecting ribs before the planks were attached. But at the moment few other archaeologists would accept this as more than an interesting guess.

As well as its combined 'shell' and 'skeleton' technique, another feature of the Yassi Ada ship dictated by its period was its length to width ratio. Its hull was some seventeen feet across at its widest, giving a ratio of 3·6 to 1. This is decidedly streamlined for a cargo vessel. Yet long before the Yassi Ada ship was found the Yale historian, Robert S. Lopez, had suggested that in the troubled times of the seventh century AD ships would have been built smaller and faster so that they could dodge or outrun the hostile or piratical vessels which lurked on every route. So here was archaeology confirming historical theory.

Another interesting feature of the ship was the galley, which was aft and set as low in the hull as possible, though its roof stood up higher than the main deck. Thanks to the careful plotting of every object in the cargo and cabin area, van Doorninck was able to work out almost exactly where its front bulkhead was, and that its roof was tiled. Similar tiles had been found on other earlier Roman wrecks by divers, but no one before had recorded their position carefully enough to tell what their purpose had been, or why there were sometimes two sorts, some heavy and some light. Now van Doorninck could show that the light tiles were for the roof of the galley and the heavy ones for the hearth.

The galley was well equipped. Besides the tiled stove with iron bars, and a roof-tile with a hole in it to let out the smoke, there had been a cupboard represented by a bronze handle, and shelves which held eight large red plates, two cups, three jars with spouts and eighteen resin-lined pitchers for drinking wine. Also stowed in the galley were twenty-two round-bottomed cooking pots, two copper cauldrons, a large water jar, and seventeen assorted storage jars. Then there was a purse or two which Bass suspects held the ship's victualling money; this consisted of 54 copper coins called *folles* and sixteen gold coins, together worth just a little more than seven *solidi*, the standard unit of the time.

Both labour and food were cheap at this time. Though a cloak might cost one to three *solidi*, a blacksmith's or shipwright's wages for a year would be about eight *solidi*, of which five would keep him in food for a year. So Bass calculates the money aboard would

The Yassi Ada ship may have been something like this ship from a sixth-century AD mosaic in the Church of Sant' Appollinare Nuovo, Ravenna.

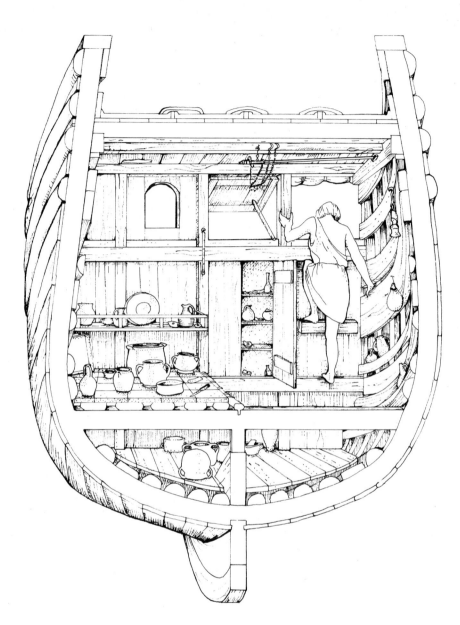

An artist's conjectural impression of how the galley of the Yassi Ada ship may have looked.

have fed a crew of fifteen for a month with something left over for emergencies.

All these fairly elaborate arrangements for cooking on board contrast with those of the Kyrenia ship, which appeared to have no means of heating food on board; Katzev suspects they took their cauldron ashore and heated it when possible, and when it wasn't possible, as with the Vikings, it was cold food on board. But at least the Greeks and Romans had plenty of wine, where the Vikings merely had dried fish and the consolation that if they

52

chewed dry raw grain it swelled in the stomach and a handful would ease hunger more than one might expect.

In a late Roman wreck found at Torre Sgarrata in southern Italy, remains of bones of sheep, cattle and pigs show that the crew didn't eat too badly on board, once cooking arrangements came into existence.

The Yassi Ada ship was well equipped in ways other than its galley. The anchors were an example: there were no fewer than eleven of them, three large, two intermediate, and six small. There are two possible reasons for this large number. The practical one was that although Julius Caesar had recorded with surprise that the Venetii of Brittany used chain cables on their anchors in the first century BC, in the Mediterranean in the seventh century AD they were evidently still being secured by ropes. This probably meant both that they were easily lost and that more than one might be needed at a time, as they lacked any weight of chain to make them hold more securely on the sea-bed. The other reason could have been that every ship was required by law to have a certain number of different sizes of anchor.

When the anchors were brought to the surface, they were largely shapeless lumps of concretion. However, after a good deal of experiment, the excavators found the best way of dealing with this concretion of sand and shells which builds up on the sea-bed round iron. The technique was to cut into the concretion with a diamond-edge rotary jeweller's saw, wash out the mushy iron oxide which was all that remained of the original iron object, then take a cast from the inside of the concretion. Variations of this technique have long been known. The contorted bodies of humans and dogs from Pompeii, where lava rather than concretion embodied the original shapes, are possibly the best known examples.

The difference at Yassi Ada was that instead of the usual brittle plaster they used a synthetic rubber compound. This produced unbreakable, firm but pliable casts, and with their surfaces coloured by the remaining iron oxide, they gave a very good impression indeed of a slightly rusty version of the original objects.

Using this method on a large but unpromising collection of bits of concretion, Michael Katzev was able to recreate the boatswain's tool chest, double-headed axes, pickaxes, a hoe, a shovel, bill-hooks, a pruning hook, and hammers, knives, punches, gouges, files, chisels, bits, and many nails. 'Such implements,' Katzev writes, 'vividly illustrate the independent nature of Byzantine

Three of the twenty terracotta oil lamps found on board the Yassi Ada ship.

The two-man sub-
marine, the *Asherah*,
with the frame
attached to its hull
which held the two
aerial survey cameras.

merchant ships, capable of landing at well-protected coves to replenish their firewood or cut timber to refit some part of the ship damaged in storm.'

We know at least two members of the ship's complement by name. One, whose name was stamped on the magnificent bronze 'steel-yard' beam-balance, was 'Georgios the Elder, owner/sea captain'. He may have shared the cost of the thirty-seven tons of cargo, worth perhaps three hundred gold *solidi*, with Ioannes, or John, whose name was on a lead seal, and who may have been a merchant, or merchant's agent.

Both the coins and the pottery found aboard suggest a northern origin for the craft, as do the handful of dark, gleaming Bosphorus mussels, which the cook certainly had not collected anywhere near the site of the sinking. Possibly the ship's home port was in the Hellespont itself. From there, in Bass's view, it was sailing southward with its cargo of empty amphorae towards the celebrated wine-producing centres of Kos, Knidos and Rhodes, when disaster struck so suddenly that the crew, unlike the luckier Kyrenia people, did not have time to rescue all their personal valuables.

Though not particularly well-preserved, the Yassi Ada ship

has made an important contribution both to our knowledge of the development of ship-building and the history of the seventh century AD just because she was treated as she would have been if found on land by archaeologists. Nevertheless the operation was a time-consuming one, and already the University Museum of Pennsylvania has pointed the way of further developments with its miniature two-man submarine, the *Asherah*. This was built by the Electric Boat Division of General Dynamics and was the first non-military submarine made in the company's sixty-year history. Fitted with a pair of modified aerial survey cameras mounted six feet (1·83 metres) apart, it is designed to take pairs of stereo-photographs on command from its pilot. It was tried out on the fourth-century Roman wreck lying nearby at Yassi Ada in 140 feet (42·7 metres) of water. Divers watching saw the little inner-space ship turn onto course and then the great stroboscopic lights flashed in rhythm as she made her pass over the wreck. A second pass and the underwater part of the planning was done. Fifty-six hours of laboratory work was needed subsequently, but in less than an hour under water an accurate survey of the amphorae cargo had been made. With the methods used on the Byzantine wreck, this would have taken a dozen aqualung divers many months. The way to the future had been clearly demonstrated.

6

Stone Age Sailors:
Pig-bones on the Beach

In 1946 a tidal wave struck the Pacific island of Nuku Hiva in the Marquesas group. On the remote and isolated beach of Ha'atuatua it neatly sliced off the sand dunes, leaving them piled in a thirty-foot-high bank seventy yards (64 metres) back from the shore. Ten years later, Robert Suggs, a graduate of Columbia University, New York, who was making an archaeological reconnaissance of the island for the American Museum of Natural History, rode out of the hibiscus bush onto the broad sand flats of the beach. He had been drawn there, driving his tired shaggy horse along the milky mud paths of the mountainous interior, past endless waterfalls, by rumours of a quantity of pig-bones that were said to lie in a long stretch on the beach. As he rode along, the sand was entirely still and deserted except for the endless foaming ranks of Pacific rollers and a few herons.

According to Suggs, when at last he saw the reputed pig-bones, he nearly fell out of his saddle. Not pigs but human beings had been their origin. Ribs, thighs, vertebrae and innumerable smaller bones were everywhere, even an almost complete upside-down skull. They appeared to have come from a thick black band in the sand, perhaps twenty inches (fifty cms) deep, rich with the dark detritus of human occupation—ash, charcoal, rotted rubbish, pieces of stone, coral and shell tools, and large cobbles set together in some sort of pavement. Above and below this stained layer the sand was clean and white, showing that whoever had left this debris had eventually moved on, leaving nature to cover everything with its cleansing layers of sand, until the tidal wave had ripped these away and revealed what lay beneath. Since then the wind had kept sweeping the

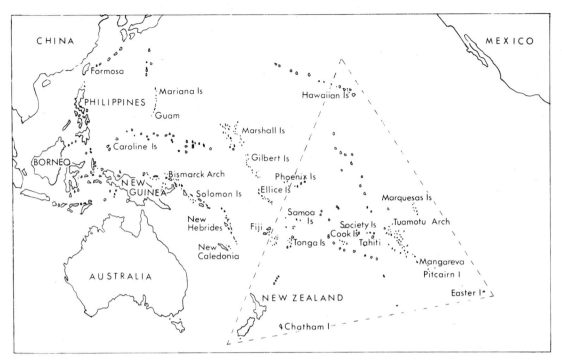

The Pacific Ocean, showing the triangle in which the islands of Polynesia lie.

sand away so that the compact dark layer lay exposed in many places for several square feet, with its scattered contents of bones and stone and shell lying exactly where they had fallen originally.

Suggs's photographs, some samples from hastily dug pits and his report to Dr Shapiro of the American Museum of Natural History resulted in him returning the following year with his wife and John Belmont, a Harvard anthropology student. Their aim was to try to excavate the beach site properly, and some other sites inland which Suggs's reconnaissance had also discovered.

His brief investigation of the beach at Ha'atuatua the year before had shown that the main concentration of domestic tools and refuse was round a river-mouth, suggesting that this was where the original occupants' houses had been grouped. In the centre of the beach, on a slight rise, had been the main burial ground. Trenches were laid down to examine both these areas, and inside the trenches a series of squares measuring five by four feet (1·52 by 1·22 metres) were dug down to the clean sand below the occupation layer. The first few squares yielded little, beyond the odd piece of broken tool. Then a dark blotch appeared which developed into the top of a covered refuse pit. This too yielded nothing specific. Further on, smaller dark patches revealed themselves as post-holes where stones from the beach had been laid to support the feet of wooden

57

posts for huts which had long since rotted away.

As they worked down towards the sea, carefully sieving the excavated sand to extract any small objects in it, Suggs's attention was suddenly caught by something of a different texture to the pebbles being shaken in the sieve by one of his Marquesan helpers. Suggs doubted his own eyes as he searched for what he had glimpsed —a brick-red fragment looking like pottery. Native pottery had never been known in Eastern Polynesia; the nearest places where pottery had been used in ancient times were Tonga in the west and Ecuador to the east, both several thousand miles across the ocean. Yet here was a piece of pottery at almost the lowest level of strata that had been laid down by some long-past occupation of this Marquesan beach. Hardly had he examined this particular piece when another larger one appeared. Deep down in a post-hole nearer the sea, yet a third piece turned up. This time it was a bit from the rim of a pot with a grooved lip. Suggs's Marquesan helpers could not at first understand his excitement. Many of the tools found in the excavation were familiar to them from their modern equivalents, but pottery was entirely new to them. The nearest equivalents they could think of were the stoneware bottles which contained officially-forbidden absinthe and Kümmel; so *hue kea* or 'stone container' was the name they gave to these scraps which were about to change the generally-held concepts of Marquesan prehistory.

A new trench at right angles to the first one soon produced another excitement, as well as more post-holes and empty pits. This was a brown human bone sticking out of the sand. Carefully brushing away the sand, Suggs first revealed a heavy collarbone and then a shoulder blade. In the socket where the upper arm-bone should have fitted, though, there was nothing. More brushing revealed the rib-cage and then the reason for the missing arm. In a shallow pit had been laid a headless, limbless male torso. Flecks of charcoal round the body and shiny splotches on the bones suggested the reason for this macabre sight. Here lay the victim of a cannibal feast.

Later finds revealed a different and marginally less macabre practice. These consisted of three female skulls with the middle teeth of the upper and lower jaws removed. This suggested that these might have been 'ancestor' or 'trophy' skulls. These were first cleaned after the flesh had dried, then the lower jaws were tied to the skulls with cords passing through the gaps where the teeth had been. The final process was to cover the whole skull with bark cloth which was painted to resemble a face. These re-created heads were then hung in the house or carried round at important ceremonies.

By and large, the evidence from the burials agreed with eighteenth- and nineteenth-century reports of the traditional mortuary customs of the Marquesans. One exception was a complete dog-burial, as it was commonly thought that this animal had been introduced to the islands by Europeans.

Other evidence these ancient human bones produced was a frequent bony growth on the surface of the joints. Young and old skeletons alike produced these. Evidently the early Marquesans had suffered badly from arthritis. Probably the cool and damp Marquesan nights had largely contributed to this.

Sometimes the objects buried with the bones threw light on how the early Marquesans lived. These offerings were often food, such as pieces of pig or fish. There was no great variety in the amount of food in different graves, so evidently there was little social distinction between them. Only occasionally did something exceptional appear, like a necklace of forty-eight carefully perforated whales' teeth.

A better understanding grew, too, of these people's religious life as the excavation proceeded. A stone kerb some twenty inches (fifty cms) high was found to have edged a pavement at the very earliest level and in this had been set single-stone pillars, one of which was still standing. Such simple temples had been regarded as the earliest known in Eastern Polynesia, but none like this had ever been found before in the Marquesas.

Another rarity was the carvings found on a flat surface of bed-rock, once the coralline deposit on top had been cleared away. Some of these may have been related to specific events, like the carving of a sperm whale, whose stranding on the island might have been both a memorable event and provided the large whale bones scattered around the site.

Despite the idyllic appearance of its surroundings—burnished sand, glittering sea, mountains softly changing from green to blue—the beach of Ha'atuatua was by no means a paradise for the excavators. Apart from the heat, the chief drawback was the hordes of fiercely-biting *nono* flies, which made everyone make sure they had tied their shirts very securely at waist and neck and their trousers at the ankles. Even modern insect repellents did not deter them. Suggs once counted eighty flies on his hands that had bitten there before

Rock carvings including one of a sperm whale, from Nuku Hiva.

OPPOSITE
Excavating on Nuku
Hiva, Marquesas
Islands.

dying a sticky chemical death. When the situation got really intolerable, one of the Marquesans would run down to the high-water mark, collect some driftwood and start a large bonfire among the green hibiscus bushes at the top of the beach. The dead leaves there gave off clouds of bitter grey smoke which drove the flies off, but usually ended by sending the choking and half-blinded excavators upwind into clear air, where the flies at once got to work again.

Nevertheless, by their persistence and subsequent analysis, the excavators were building up a vivid and detailed picture, not just of a piece of ancient human history, but of an important moment in what is probably ancient man's greatest maritime achievement—the first human occupation of the empty islands of the Pacific by a people using only a Stone Age technology, Stone Age boats, and what we might once have been tempted to call, rather patronisingly, primitive navigation. Thanks to the information extracted by Suggs from the black band on his beach, we now have an extremely good idea of how these extraordinary sea-farers were equipped, what cargoes they brought with them, and what they did at the testing moment when they first beached their canoes on an unoccupied group of islands like the Marquesas.

The ten volcanic islands of the Marquesas archipelago lie nine degrees south of the equator on the extreme eastern edge of Polynesia, some 3,000 miles from Australia and 3,000 from South America. Their lofty green mountain peaks, slashed with red where erosion removed grass, fern and palm to reveal the clayey soil underneath, were first seen by European eyes in AD 1595 when a Spanish expedition under Admiral Mendana which had sailed from Callao arrived there *en route* to conquer the Solomon Islands. As soon as they discovered there was no gold or jewels to be had, the Spaniards, after a brief interval of slaughter of the local inhabitants, moved on. Two centuries later, Captain Cook anchored there. He was interested in more scientific matters, though he too had brushes with the local people. In 1842 the islands were occupied by the French and within less than a century the 100,000 Marquesans had been reduced by smallpox, venereal disease (often brought in by deserters from whaling ships), alcohol and other European scourges to a dispirited 1,500 or so. All around them lay the decaying remains of their pre-European past—ruined house platforms, temples and pavements, littered with stone axes, carved stone pestles, and skulls, while up in the hills, defensive mounds and

trenches were scattered with the polished sling-stone missiles of their own inter-tribal wars; so much so that one anthropologist said that any excavation was quite unnecessary there, because so much was available on the surface!

Nevertheless, there were also many unanswered questions. Guesses as to when the first inhabitants of the Marquesas had arrived there varied from 1000 BC to AD 1400. Their suggested origins ranged from China to Mexico. And no one had any idea at all when and how the ancient stone monuments of the islands had evolved.

Thanks to the work of the American Museum of Natural History's expedition, we can now answer many of these questions. Radio-carbon dates suggest that the first occupants of Ha'atuatua probably arrived there about 120 BC, though other authorities would prefer a date some four or five hundred years later. They came in two or three canoes, which were part of a larger group that scattered to find homes throughout the islands. After choosing their landing site, they built low boat-shaped houses round the stream-mouth. These decayed quite quickly and were frequently rebuilt. Nearby they built a small temple within which was an altar. Round this they buried their dead. The burials tell us that these people were Polynesians, with all the physical traits that distinguished that race. The graves also suggested that they practised ceremonial cannibalism and ancestor-worship, and had little difference in status amongst themselves.

With them in their canoes they brought pigs, dogs, and, no doubt unintentionally, rats, because the bones of all three were found in the tell-tale layer of black sand. Fish and shellfish were an obvious item of food for such great sea-farers as the Polynesians, and the evidence of the thousands of fishbones and shells was supplemented by the finding of many fish-hooks, notably one-piece ones made from mother-of-pearl shell, and composite ones for catching bonito.

Other tool finds added to the details of their diet. For instance, narrow saw-toothed blades of mother-of-pearl were a common find, and they were used to scrape the inside of a half-coconut to produce long shreds of white meat which were then squeezed to produce the milk. Then there were snail-shells in which a sharp-edged hole had been made; these were used as scrapers on the sides of taro roots to pare off a sliver of skin which emerged through the mouth of the snail-shell. The interesting thing about these is that they are not at all like the cowrie-shell peelers which have been

Pearl-shell fish-hooks found by Robert Suggs on Nuku Hiva.

used by the Marquesans ever since they were first observed by Europeans. On the other hand these snail-shell scrapers are just like ones used in Fiji and New Caledonia, thousands of miles to the west. Like the pottery, they pointed to the distant west as the original home of the Marquesans, as did some of the polished stone adzes and a peculiar type of circular disc made of pearl shell which was used as a head-dress.

So we can say that these daring canoeists brought with them coconuts and breadfruit as well as root crops like taro and yam to supplement their diet of fish, shellfish and pork because none of these plants grow naturally here. They were definitely Polynesian in physical type and they came to the Marquesas from an island in Western Polynesia, which was either in close touch with Melanesia even more to the west or still shared much of its culture. In particular they came from a high volcanic island rather than a flat coral atoll, because their tool kit and knowledge of raw materials showed complete familiarity with those sorts of conditions.

In other words, at a period somewhere between the Kyrenia and Yassi Ada ships, and probably before the Romans left Britain around AD 400, these Polynesian sailors were ranging thousands of miles across the Pacific in well-equipped expeditions that were perfectly capable of colonising uninhabited groups of islands, even though technologically they were at least fifteen hundred years behind Roman Britons and were still in the Stone Age.

No actual canoe part survived in that black band in the sand, but from the tools found there, as well as from the reports of the first Europeans in Polynesia and recent anthropological studies, it is possible to get a very good idea of what they were like. There were three basic types—the single canoe, the outrigger canoe, and the great double canoe, or catamaran, with a platform between its two hulls. The basic member was always a long log, hollowed out, usually by burning and then chipping away the burnt wood with stone axes or shells. 'We have two tools,' said one old canoe-builder, 'the adze and fire.'

To this basic dug-out member were attached bow and stern pieces and sometimes additional strakes, always by lashings, which in some cases were countersunk in grooves, and sometimes taken over battens running along the join. On islands where the coconut palm grew, this cord was made from soaked discarded coconut fibres. While the crews sat gossiping in the canoe-huts, they would always be rolling little bunches of coconut fibre together

63

Some of the ancient stone ruins in the centre of Nuku Hiva.

between their bare thighs and hands until it was a hard strand. Then in turn these strands would be twisted together to make rope that was strong, resistant to rot, and with a third useful quality as well—a surface bristling with stiff sticking-out little hairs. They were hard on the hands, but they also meant that a knot or lashing hardly ever slipped; a simple half-hitch would hold almost anything. In New Zealand, a form of flax was used instead of this coconut fibre.

Throughout the Pacific, until recent times, every aspect of canoe-building was closely tied to religious practice. All sorts of rituals and restrictions had to be observed to keep off bad luck. Sometimes the builders even had to refrain from all sexual activity, because this might have a bad effect on the gods' disposition.

Because they had very large trees available, the Maoris of New Zealand gradually abandoned the use of the outrigger: but in most parts of the Pacific it was a crucial device. Thomas Gladwin, Visiting Professor of Anthropology at Harvard University, has made a special study of canoe-building and navigation techniques on Pulawat, a relatively unspoilt island in the Carolines group, and his tribute to their craft is uncompromising:

'The beating which the complex structure of a sailing canoe can take in a heavy storm is severe. It is driven by wind, smashed by the running seas, wrenched upward and dropped steeply down again on the crests and in the troughs of waves which come in from all angles. That it survives at all is remarkable. That it survives so well is a tribute not only to careful construction and maintenance but also to a remarkably sophisticated and rational basic design.'

The advantages of an outrigger or a double canoe, which is virtually just a larger equivalent, have been demonstrated recently in contemporary European and American catamarans. The weight of the outrigger is used to balance the thrust of the wind on the sail. On a fore-and-aft rigged yacht, this is done by the width of the hull and the weight and depth of the keel. Both of these mean that a bigger wave is pushed in front of the boat, and therefore more energy is used to overcome the drag. By not relying on hull-width or a keel for stability, the outrigger canoe can have a much smaller body, with much less drag.

The outrigger has one disadvantage. Because it is usually kept to windward, it is generally impossible to tack in the normal way. Instead the craft changes ends, as it were, the sail and rigging are carried aft, and it sets off with the stern now becoming the bow. But the drawbacks of this operation are more than compensated for by the other advantages of the outrigger.

Another interesting detail which confirms the skill of these Pacific boat builders is the canoe's bow. Unlike the underneath of the hull, which usually has a superb aerodynamic shape—a tribute to the eye of the master-builder who shaped it with only his inherited skill and a measuring string to guide him—the bows often look blunt and asymmetrical. In the view of the Pulawat builders, however, this makes little difference to performance. It is only recently that tank and model tests in the United States and Europe have confirmed this, and shown that the very small bow-wave produced by the Pulawat sailing canoe's blunt bow is no accident!

It is revealing, too, to see what these Pacific craftsmen have absorbed and adapted from European techniques of ship-building. Perhaps the most important is the material for sails. Sail-cloth

65

E

is more efficient, lasts longer, is lighter and handles more easily than the traditional woven pandanus leaves.

Then there is the compass. One would think that this vital device, taken together with the all-wood construction of Pacific canoes, would be an ideal acquisition. It is in fact used—but not as we would use it, as the chief means for setting a course. Their use for it is simply to hold steady on a course which they have already worked out from their own elaborate star compass, which every navigator, after years of instruction and committing to memory, has clearly in his mind's eye. The compass is also useful to keep track of the direction of drift if they are caught out in a storm.

There is a curious link between the skill of these Pacific navigators and the ancient inhabitants of the British Isles. Both built megaliths, those great stone structures like Stonehenge and Avebury. The Pacific ones were not as large or elaborate, but they were still megaliths. Neither people could read or write, so, in the phraseology of archaeology, they were barbarians. Yet both had an extraordinary knowledge of astronomy. In fact the people most likely to find it easy to accept the arguments of Professor Alexander Thom—that the builders of stone circles in the British Isles in the second millennium BC were skilled theoretical astronomers—are those familiar with Melanesian and Polynesian navigation techniques. Both Pacific navigators and stone circle builders committed to memory vast amounts of knowledge, acquired over long periods of time, without the help of writing. Both knew the night sky like the back of their hands. Both had elaborate theoretical concepts. Or so it seems. In fact the groups of young men on a Pacific island, sitting round an ancient master navigator or 'water-eater' as the great ones were called, learning star courses by means of a ring of pebbles in the sand, may be the nearest we will ever get to appreciating the sort of way Stonehenge was planned, if we substitute Bronze Age British astronomer-priest for Stone Age Polynesian navigator.

Rather more modern priests and missionaries from Britain and other western countries have had another and quite unexpected impact on Pacific sea travel. When iron tools were first obtained from the Spaniards in the eighteenth century, smoothing off the hull became easier than with the previous stone tools. More recently Christianity did away with the taboos and rituals associated with canoe-building. This meant more men could lend a hand with the

A seventeenth-century European impression of a double canoe.

tedious and time-consuming job of removing every small bump and roughness on the surface of the hull. So thanks to the missionaries, the canoes now slip even faster through the water.

Knowing through modern studies the brilliant qualities of the often crude-looking Pacific canoes, and the skills of their navigators, excavations like those at Nuku Hiva complete a picture for us which before was virtually only legend. Captain Cook and the other first Europeans in the Pacific were rightly astonished at the great double canoes, with the cosy thatched hut on the platform between, the tubs of fermented breadfruit paste and nets of coconuts for food, the gourds of water for drinking supply. Some of these could carry up to a hundred people and were even longer than Captain Cook's own *Endeavour*. How and when the vast reaches of the Pacific were overcome in the past, in vessels like these and in big outriggers, is no longer a mystery. Technically, archaeologists would call their crews barbarians; but every additional piece of information produced by anthropologists and archaeologists like Suggs increases one's admiration for them, even if some of them were cannibals as well as great sailors.

7

Viking Ships: the Eight-cowhide Craft

The Scandinavians have a long and honourable tradition of experimental nautical archaeology—of excavating ancient ships found in the soil, and building and sailing replicas of them to throw greater light on the seafaring achievements of the past. Most of the major ship discoveries made in Scandinavia have now been given this extra dimension of practical knowledge; but in 1971, a Norwegian boat-builder called Odd Johnsen went even further. He built a boat that no one had tried to build, or even seen, for perhaps 2,500 years —a boat of which not a trace remained except for innumerable ancient carvings on rock-faces in Norway: and eight-cowhide Bronze Age boat.

The tradition of making replicas began in 1893, when Captain Magnus Andersen of Norway carried out a remarkable experimental sea-voyage—sailing a replica of a Viking longship across the Atlantic from Norway to New York.

But Captain Andersen's journey had really started twenty-six years before. It was in 1867 that the owners of a farm on the east side of Oslo fjord began to cart away earth from a large mound on a slope leading down to the River Glomma, some sixteen miles north of Frederikstad and Odd Johnsen's boatyard. The mound had been dug into before, but this occasion was exceptional because they came upon the timbers of a large ship. By the time archaeologists from Oslo University had arrived, a large part of the vessel had been uncovered. The ship had been placed lying north/south and on ground level, and then the mound, which was 280 feet (85·5 metres) in diameter and the second largest in Norway, had been raised over it. A square burial chamber in the stern had held the charred bones of a man and a horse, but by the time the archae-ologists arrived, the wood had begun to disintegrate and little remained to preserve from the Tune ship, as it is called, except a wooden spade, a hand spike and a few pieces of wood. In any case the mound had also clearly been plundered in antiquity as well as dug into in more recent times.

The much better known Gokstad ship was a rather different case. On the west side of Oslo fjord, on a flat treeless plain, there stood another large mound, in which, according to legend, a king had been buried with all his treasure. In 1880, some locals started to dig into it, but this time the digging was stopped until archaeologists could get to the scene, and so a proper and remarkable excavation took place. The prow of the ship was found on the second day and the whole operation finished in two and a half months. After that the vessel was taken to Oslo. Since this was before the days of motor vehicles, the seventy-six-foot-long (23-metre) ship, sawn in two halves, finished its journey on a large cart drawn by many horses. It must indeed have been an impressive sight moving through the Oslo streets, and even in those days caused a memorable traffic jam.

Unlike the Tune ship, the Gokstad ship had had a grave dug for it. Fortunately the diggers chose a site on blue clay, which was largely responsible for its remarkable state of preservation. It too had a burial chamber built over it, and in this was found the body of a king lying in his finest clothes on a bed with his weapons beside him. His skeleton showed him to have been a well-built man, five feet ten inches tall, and some fifty years of age. Also in the ship were three small rowing boats, all as well and elegantly built as the larger one, many eating and drinking utensils, and a huge bronze cauldron which the crew, like that of the Kyrenia ship, evidently only used for heating their food when they were on shore. Twelve horses and six dogs had been buried in the grave at the same time, but while they were placed outside the ship, the body of a peacock had been laid inside. This mound too had been broken into in the past, the robbers making a hole in the port side of the ship and the burial chamber, so only scraps of the smaller and more ornamental objects, like bits of silk worked with gold thread, remained. The robbers had also left behind a piece of a board which could be used for playing a different sort of game on each side.

The Oseberg ship, which was dug out of another mound in 1903, was even better preserved. Set on a bottom level of blue clay, it had then been covered with stones and finally hermetically sealed with a layer of peat, an ideal combination for preserving wood. Unfortunately the weight of the stones had counterbalanced this to some extent, causing the ship to sink into the clay unevenly and break up. It had therefore to be lifted in many pieces. These were boiled in alum and then impregnated with linseed oil. When reconstructed, they showed that this vessel had been a sort of royal yacht, elaborately carved and decorated. In the burial chamber this time were the bodies of two women; the younger one, of thirty or so, was assumed to be a slave girl, while the older woman of sixty or seventy who was very badly crippled by arthritis, was believed to be a queen. The female nature of this burial gave a rather different emphasis to the contents. There were quilts, pillows, blankets, tapestries, clothing, scissors and kitchen equipment, a stool and a chair, which had once had a plaited rope seat. Larger objects included a four-wheeled cart and a sledge. In conformity with the others, thirteen horses, three dogs and an ox had been buried with the queen, and robbers had been there as well, this time getting in through the roof of the burial chamber.

Once again, the objects they had ignored were as interesting in their way as the possible gold and jewellery which they may have taken. There were about fifty wild apples of two sorts (some of whose flesh and skin actually still survived), cress seeds, woad for dyeing things blue, walnuts and hazel nuts. From all these it was possible to tell that the burial took place in late August or early September.

Two of these three Viking ships have now been fully restored and reconstructed and can be seen in the Viking Ship Museum in Oslo. Their marvellous lines alone make them worth a visit, quite apart from the many fascinating pieces of equipment, from oars and gangplanks to anchors, which go with them.

The outstanding characteristics of these ships are the keels and their flexibility. The keel is made of a single oak plank upright on edge. This gave both great strength and the ability to sail to windward, which previous northern ships had lacked. The elasticity was due to the fact that the nineteen frames, or ribs and cross-beams, were not fastened to the keel at all and were only lashed to holes in cleats in the planks where the planks had been left thicker. This technique gave great lightness and flexibility. A stiffer method would have required greater strength and heaviness overall. There

The excavation of the Oseberg ship.

were sixteen planks each side, clinker built, or rivetted together through the overlaps and caulked with animal hair. The skill of the builders is well reflected in the difference between these sixteen planks. The tenth strake up from the keel, for instance, which was where the waterline came, was the thickest and strongest of all. The fourteenth up, in which the holes for the oars came, was the next thickest. Above this were two light ones which were attached to a strong gunwhale. The oarports could be sealed from inside by movable flaps.

The mast was very cunningly mounted in a socket in a large swelling block of wood set along the keel. This was called the 'old crone' in Norse. Above this was the mast partner which had a large cleft in it along its aftermost end. This meant the mast could be raised or lowered very easily.

The cunning skill of all these devices and details was put to the test again in 1893, on the four hundredth anniversary of the discovery of the American continent by Christopher Columbus. The Great Chicago Exhibition was being held to commemorate the occasion, and the Norwegians decided that the pioneer voyages of their

71

ancestors, who had previously discovered North America (Vinland), should not be forgotten. Their contribution was the brain-child of Captain Magnus Andersen, who as a former sailing skipper and current editor of a shipping paper was well qualified to organise both the sea-going side of the scheme and the publicity for it. The idea was to build an exact replica of the Gokstad ship and sail it across the North Atlantic to the Exhibition.

The replica was built at Sandefjord of Norwegian oak, except for the keel. No tree of the necessary size for that could be found in Norway, so in the end they were reduced to importing a huge Canadian oak specifically for that one purpose. The same problem arose with the mast partner, but finally a large enough tree was found on a farm not far from Gokstad itself, and the need to import another tree was avoided.

The ship was launched on February 19th 1893, from the Framnes shipyard, and although it looked splendidly graceful and effective, there were plenty of pessimists who said that trying to cross the Atlantic in it was a dangerous risk to life. Fortunately the combined traditional skills of the Vikings and Captain Andersen proved them wrong. The replica left Marstein near Bergen on April 30th and arrived in Newfoundland safely twenty-seven days later.

Her crew met a good deal of bad weather on the way, but the replica took it in her stride. The characteristic the modern sailors found most unusual, because it was so alien to later shipbuilding traditions, was the flexibility. In Captain Andersen's words:

'The bottom of the ship was an object of primary interest. As will be remembered, it was fastened to the ribs with withy, below the crossbeams. The bottom, as well as the keel, could therefore yield to the movement of the ship, and in a heavy head sea it would rise and fall as much as three-quarters of an inch (two cms). But strangely enough the ship was watertight all the same. Its elasticity was apparent also in other ways. In a heavy sea the gunwhale would twist up to six inches (fifteen cms) out of line. All this elasticity, combined with the fine lines, naturally made for speed, and we often had the pleasure of darting through the water at speeds of ten, and sometimes even eleven knots.'

And remember, this was with a single square sail!

Another tribute to her lines was that until she reached a speed of more than three to four knots, she left practically no wake at all behind her.

72

The replica of the Gokstad ship moored in Chicago for the Exhibition of 1893 after its successful crossing of the Atlantic.

What speed she would have achieved with her thirty-two oars alone was never really tested. There had been plans to row her up to her berth in New York on arrival there, and student volunteers had been taken aboard for the purpose, but evidently they found the conditions rather different from that of their racing shells, and there seems to have been something of a shambles. Fortunately there was a favourable wind, so an elegant arrival at her New York berth under sail did not in any way mar the achievement of the crossing. The most successful piece of rowing seems to have been done by Norwegian members of the Milwaukee sailors' association, who took her up the river of that name as though, in Captain Andersen's words, 'every one had had a long experience of Viking raids'.

This voyage is one of the strongest confirmations that the people of the past, within the limitations of the materials available to them and the circumstances in which they lived, could often produce, just through experience and natural ability, as effective and artistic results as we with all our contemporary gadgetry.

However, the Gokstad ship was only one of the many kinds used by the Scandinavians in their great period of expansion between the eighth and eleventh centuries AD. During this time they were to be

73

found from the Arctic North Cape to Sicily and from Byzantium to Vinland, or North America. In the course of all this they carried out the early Middle Ages' most remarkable piece of colonisation, the settlement of Iceland and parts of Greenland. Most of this was done and supported, not by dragon-prowed, striped-sailed longships, but by *knörrs*. These were the round-bowed hard-working merchantmen, the 'ocean-striding sea-bison' in the Norsemen's phrase.

The process through which we know what one of these looked like began in 1956 when two Danish amateur frogmen, Aa. Skjelberg and H. Conradsen, salvaged an oak frame from the sea-bed of Roskilde fjord in Denmark and brought it to the National Museum in Copenhagen. It had formed part of a barrier on the sea-bed across a channel leading towards the town of Roskilde, the old capital of Denmark. This obstruction on the sea-bed had been known locally for some time as 'Queen Margarethe's ship' after one of the better known rulers of the Danish early Middle Ages.

Examination showed that the frame did not come from that period but from the earlier Viking age. This was enough to set off a more thorough underwater examination of the barrier. This revealed, during 1957 and 1958, that not one but at least four ships had been scuttled there (the final total was five). That meant a large-scale rescue operation would be well worthwhile, in spite of the difficulties. The visibility under water was very poor, the nails of the ships had rusted away to nothing, the wood was soft, and strong currents would carry away anything that became loosened. So it was decided to build a cofferdam round the whole area, drain it, and excavate the whole barrier of ships, which had originally been reinforced with stones and posts, evidently to stop raiding craft using the channel. This very expensive salvage operation was financed by a number of organisations and trusts, in particular one whose wealth comes from a fortunately widespread thirst for Danish beer.

The cofferdam eventually enclosed an irregular five-sided area. Its sheetpiling was normally driven ten feet (three metres) into the ground, though it was set deeper where there was more stress on it. By 1962 the dam was complete and on July 6th the excavation started. It was clear from the beginning that the water would have to be pumped out very carefully, for as the water level went down, the stones in the ships would lose some of their buoyancy, which would put extra weight on the ships and could well break them up or distort them. Also of course there would be the familiar danger of waterlogged wood drying out and then disintegrating. So the

74

Aerial view of the cofferdam surrounding the excavation of the Roskilde ships.

water was pumped out a little at a time, until a level of stones and sand was revealed. This was then cleared and more pumping done until the next layer appeared, and so on.

Soon the excavators reached the bottom of the fjord, and when this had been cleared of algae, they were faced with a sandy plain across which stretched a long low ridge which contained the ships. Excavating them provided many problems. The wreckage was far too vulnerable to be trodden on, so they made a series of movable plank catwalks which could be placed over the part on which they were working. On these the excavators, usually from six to fourteen students at a time, knelt or lay on their stomachs to deal with the vessels beneath them. The tools they used were not those of a normal excavation either. Anything of metal would have been far too violent in its effect. Occasionally plastic toy tools were used, but more often it was bare hands and a gentle clean-water spray with a controllable nozzle. With these they could remove in particular the sharp-edged broken shells which were present in large numbers and could very easily scratch the wood of the ships. Gradually as the shells, the stones, and the silt were removed,

75

the ships came into view. By then, a series of sprinklers had been installed to keep the newly-revealed timbers wet for twenty-four hours a day.

They had two bad crises. Once a storm raised the level of water in the fjord, and they had to put a barrier of sandbags along the top of the dam to stop the water in the fjord coming over the top. The other one was more serious—there was a short-circuit in the electrical generator, and the nineteen sprinklers stopped working. Fortunately emergency arrangements were ready. A petrol-driven motor pump on a pontoon moored outside the dam was brought into use, and together with much heaving of buckets of water, the dampness was maintained until the sprinklers were back in action again an hour later.

The sprinklers, though essential, were not popular with the excavators. They meant working in a constant seeping drizzle—and the summer was the coldest and greyest for thirty-four years! About the only time any were deliberately turned off was when photography had to take place.

Conventional recording would have been impossibly slow in the circumstances, so photogrammetry was used to make a three-dimensional record throughout. Two pairs of double cameras, which could be tilted at any angle, took many different views of every object, always including in the picture one of three reference points set up on the inside of the dam. And just as Ahmed Youssef had done with the Cheops ship, every piece of each vessel had a reference card made for it with photographs and all necessary details on it. Since every timber was also marked with a piece of plastic attached by small brass nails and with a number on it whose code showed its place of origin, it was easy to check up where any given piece came from. When the time came to start lifting the bits of the wrecks, these same numbers were also put on the plastic tubes into which the pieces of wood were put, together with a little water, before they were sealed and rafted ashore.

So efficiently was the excavation run by Ole Crumlin-Pedersen and Olof Olsen that very soon a positive conveyor-belt system was under way to record, number, lift, package and take ashore the parts of the five ships. In all, some 3,900 plastic bags of material reached the conservation centre at Brede, near Copenhagen. By October 17th the salvaging was finished and the dismantling of the cofferdam started.

Preserving wood that has been waterlogged for a long time is a difficult problem, and one that has not yet been fully solved. If the waterlogged wood is simply allowed to dry out, the damage done to the cells and their bonding in the wood by the water over the years soon takes effect and causes shrinking and distortion; this is quite apart from any damage which may have been caused by boring insects and fungi. The modern method generally used to counteract all this is to put the wood into a tank of clean water, add a fungicide, and then slowly replace the water in the tank with polyethylene glycol; this gradually drives out the water from the wood and replaces it, without changing the shape of the wood itself. Finally the polyethylene glycol sets solid in normal temperatures. But this method has its drawbacks. For one thing, it is expensive and can take a long time—some pieces of the Roskilde ships had to be kept in tanks for up to two years. Also, with very hard large pieces of oak, such as came from the celebrated Swedish ship *Wasa*, the polyethylene glycol may get through the outer layers

Piecing together the restored planking of one of the Roskilde ships.

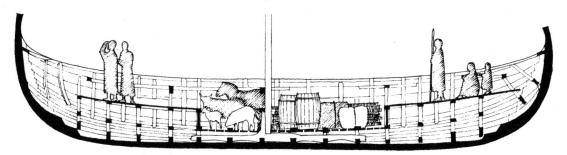

An artist's impression
of the *knörr*.

successfully but have trouble in penetrating the hard-knit centre, and this can set up distortions.

The five scuttled ships in the fjord barrier have now or are in the course of being rebuilt in the splendid museum specially constructed for them at Roskilde. Since they were deliberately sunk, they tended to be old and completely stripped of any contents. But it has been possible, by radio-carbon tests and comparisons with other Viking ships, to date them to probably somewhere between AD 950 and 1050, so they are perhaps a century later than the three famous Norwegian examples. Also, they are built more stiffly, with trenails or wooden pegs fastening the frames to the ships' sides instead of lashings. This possibly suggests that further north the ancient tradition of skin-boat building with its more flexible lashing methods survived longer, while to the south a tradition of stiffer wooden shipbuilding developed.

A piece of good fortune was that five different types of vessel were used to make the barrier at Roskilde—coasters, longships, and, above all, merchantmen. In particular, one of the merchantmen was of the large deep-sea sort which must have kept up the connection between Scandinavia, Iceland and Greenland. This craft was much broader, deeper, and heavier than a traditional longship. It also had distinct half-decks at bow and stern, and was clearly designed to be sailed most of the time, because there were only a few oar holes fore and aft, just enough perhaps to work her in and out of harbour. In the opinion of Ole Crumlin-Pedersen, now Director of the Roskilde Museum, it was undoubtedly a cargo vessel, built for carrying large loads in waters where depth did not matter.

One detail from the merchantman was of particular interest for the light it threw on the way Viking ships were sailed. This was a cleat which had clearly been designed to take what was called a *beiti-áss* in three separate positions; this was a special spar which held out the for'ard edge of the sail when beating into the wind. The discovery of the *beiti-áss* cleat made nonsense of earlier suggestions that Viking ships could only sail before the wind.

No replica has as yet been made of the Roskilde *knörr*, as this type of merchantman was called, though surely it will be one day, and so give valuable information about those voyages across the North Atlantic which the Icelandic sagas treat as casually as if they meant little more than catching a bus. But Crumlin-Pedersen has already carried out one very valuable experiment, using a replica of a longship which was found buried in the ground at Ladby in Denmark in 1935. On this sixty-foot-long (eighteen-metre) replica, which was made by Danish boy scouts in 1963, Crumlin-Pedersen fitted a copy of an oak Viking rudder which had been brought back by a fisherman from the Kattegat in 1958. The fisherman left it in his boathouse for ten days after hauling it up, but in spite of that it responded very well to conservation by the Danish National Museum. These rudders were fitted on the starboard or 'steer-board' side of Viking ships by a withy which went through a knot or 'wart' on the ship's side, through the hull and through a hole in the rudder itself. There was also a plaited leather rope round the loom higher up, holding it against the gunwhale. But basically, the rudder pivoted on the 'wart'. A tiller ran inboard at right angles to the rudder and it was this that the steersman grasped.

There had been a good deal of argument about Viking steering oars because most of the known ones are asymmetric, both in shape and thickness, and nobody quite knew why this was. The tests with the replica soon showed that, with great skill, the Vikings had found and exploited the principle of the 'balanced rudder'. This means that the rudder is so designed that when it is turned either way, the area of the blade in the water is divided into two parts, one for'ard and one aft of the turning axis. This has the effect, if the blade is properly shaped, of balancing the opposing forces on the two areas as the steering oar is turned while it moves through the water. The steersman therefore has to use very little effort to change course. Once the stern rudder was developed, about the twelfth century AD, this advantage was lost and not re-applied until the nineteenth century, though the Chinese seem to have used it even earlier than the Vikings.

In the Ladby replica, they found that even when the vessel was sailing in a strong wind, a boy scout of ten or eleven could steer it quite easily, and when it was being rowed, even if only the rowers on the starboard side pulled and tried to turn it to port, the steering oar still kept the craft easily on a straight course.

A good many ships of the Viking period, from the seventh to the

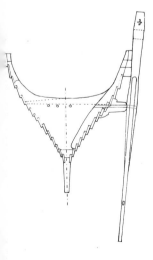

Cross-section of the Gokstad ship, showing how the steering oar was attached to its wart.

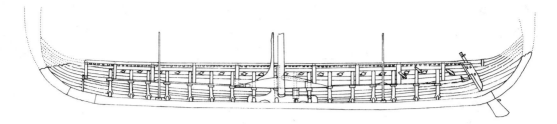

Diagrammatic side-view of the construction of the Gokstad ship, showing the mast step and mast partner.

twelfth century, have now been found. There are not so many earlier ones. Those that have been recovered we owe largely to two things—peat bogs and the sacrificial habits of the early Germanic tribes. The Roman author, Tacitus, for instance, gives a good description of part of these latter habits: 'When they meet in battle, they generally promise the spoils of war to the God of War. After the victory, captured materials are sacrificed to him and the rest of the booty is put in the same place.' The 'place' was usually a nearby lake or pond which in the course of the years might often turn into a peat bog. Peat preserves wood well, and sometimes the victors must have included captured boats as well as weapons in their offerings.

The most famous one is the Nydam craft of the fourth century AD, which was excavated from a peat bog in south Jutland in 1863. It is much cruder than the later Viking craft, has no proper keel, and appears to be built for rowing only. It was captured by the Germans when they acquired Schleswig-Holstein after the Prusso-Danish war of 1864, and a replica, which performed quite well, was rowed down the River Weser in front of Hitler in 1937.

An even earlier bog sacrifice was the Hjortspring boat. It was found in 1921 in a very small bog on the island of Als in Denmark, along with many weapons, coats of mail, wooden shields and skeletons of animals. This craft is believed to date from the Iron Age, about 300 BC. It is a light craft, made of only five planks of maple. It has no metal in it and all the pieces were joined by lashings. It has been pieced together in the National Museum of Denmark in a way which has not gone totally unchallenged. As seen today, it has the curious double ends which are often shown on Scandinavian rock carvings.

Following in the Ladby tradition, an exact replica of this vessel, correct in every detail, has been made by Danish boy scouts. This project, which started in 1971 and received much help from Ole Crumlin-Pedersen, also produced a craft which worked well, though its behaviour on the water benefitted from the addition of a little ballast.

So, all in all, Odd Johnsen had a good many predecessors when he came to tackle a Bronze Age skin boat. But he had more problems than most, too.

Odd Johnsen's boat-building shed stands on the River Glomma, Norway's equivalent to Scotland's Clyde. Across the river, vast 100,000-ton tankers are built with much clanging and banging in Norway's leading shipbuilding town, Frederikstad. But on Odd Johnsen's side of the river it is quieter, for he builds in wood: small clinker-built cabin-cruisers or fishing boats which, apart from their engines and a few other modern gadgets, go straight back, with their overlapping timbers, to the Viking ships which were surely once built in the narrow inlet next to his boathouse. On June 1st 1971, Johnsen finished off a cabin-cruiser, launched her and cleared the end of his shed for his unique task.

The design for the Bronze Age boat had been worked out by Professor Sverre Marstrander of Oslo University Museum, who had studied the rock carvings for many years. The project was being sponsored jointly by NRK the Norwegian State Broadcasting organisation and BBC 2's archaeology programme, *Chronicle*, who were going to make a film of the building and testing of the boat.

What made Odd Johnsen's task uniquely difficult was that there were no actual examples in existence to copy. He had only pictures hacked and pecked into smooth rock faces by the ancient inhabitants of Norway; and, as has often been said by nautical archaeologists, when it comes to ships, illustrations can only tell half the story, if that.

As well, these ancient pictures of boats, carved in the rocks perhaps three thousand years ago for some strange ritual reason, are the source of one of the longest-continuing controversies in Norse archaeology. Some people have thought they were wooden planked boats, others that they were dug-outs with outriggers, like the Pacific canoes. One authority even suggested they were rafts, which seems unlikely in the chilly waters of the North.

Professor Marstrander argued that the carvings represented skin boats for three main reasons. He thought the great double bows were most likely explained as protection for the hull when beaching—always a skin boat's most vulnerable moment. Secondly, the framework of a skin boat shows through its sides, both because they bulge against it and also because scraped dried skin can become almost transparent. This of course never happens with a wooden

Bronze Age carvings at Kalnes on which the replica was based. These typical Norwegian Bronze Age carvings show how the framework of the craft is visible through its sides.

81

ship because the planks cover the ribs or frames, yet in many of the rock carvings the framework can be seen perfectly clearly. Thirdly, some of the carved boats have loops outside the ends of their hulls. These would be an impossible feature in a boat made of planks. But they would easily be explained if the boat was made of flexible withies covered with skin. Then, if there were a withy sticking out of one end, it could simply be bent round back in a curve and attached to the hull again. Professor Marstrander also believes these skin boats were once part of a great prehistoric tradition of skin-boat making that stretched right round the northern hemisphere. All that was needed to make these craft was the strength to break off a few saplings, some lashings to join them together to make the hull, and some needles to sew the skins for the hull coverings. These were both simpler and more easily available to man much earlier than the polished stone axes and adzes and the good-sized trees necessary to build wooden boats. Surprisingly, too, these skin craft make excellent sea boats. The Eskimo umiak and kayak are good examples, and have survived to this day because of their effectiveness. So too are Irish curraghs and Welsh coracles, though these are now covered with tarred canvas and not the hides of cows or horses, as they once used to be. Recently a stone carving of a curragh was found at Bantry in Ireland, which dates back to the eighth century AD and shows that the design of this craft on the west coast of Ireland has hardly changed for twelve centuries. These, then, were the ideas that Professor Marstrander was putting to the test.

Odd Johnsen began his task by going out to the wood near his boathouse and cutting down eighteen young trees, mostly alders and one lime. There was no question of using seasoned timber in this case, or any form of metal fastening; wood, skin, and yards and yards of rawhide lashing were to be his only materials. He and Professor Marstrander had decided to make the bottom of the craft flat. The rock carvings, being in profile, naturally do not give any evidence on this point, so it was decided to follow the practice of Eskimo umiaks whose bottoms are made flat for ease of both loading and beaching.

The only really modern tool Odd Johnsen used was an electric drill. Otherwise he kept to an axe, a knife and a needle, though of course these were of steel, whereas his ancient predecessors would have used possibly bronze or, most of the time, stone and bone. Another question-mark was his use of wooden pegs, shaped

Odd Johnsen cutting out the cow-skin cover for the replica of the Bronze Age craft.

with his axe and then hammered in, to join some of the wooden members of the hull to each other. These joins he then wrapped round and round with rawhide lashing. There are no pegs in the Hjortspring boat, for instance; but the Eskimos have them, so it is not impossible that they were also used in the Bronze Age, which was a technologically more advanced stage than that of the Eskimos, who until they came under some European influence were a Stone Age people.

The main strength of Johnsen's vessel was the keel, to which was attached the high bow and stern. The overall length was some twenty-five feet. To the keelson inside the craft were then attached nine U-shaped frames. With the addition of gunwhales, floor timbers, stringers, and thwarts, the skeleton of the vessel was complete. The hull covering consisted of eight cowskins, cut to shape, sewn together, and then put on in one piece. This went over the edge of the gunwhales and a little way inside, and was attached by a zigzag lacing which ran continuously from holes in its edge, down round a stringer and back to the next hole in the hide. This is what the Eskimos also do and it has two advantages: it is easy to haul tight if the lacing stretches or loosens, and it gives the hide cover a shock-

83

absorbing elasticity which is very useful if the boat bumps into a piece of an ice-floe or any other obstacle.

Wherever possible, Odd Johnsen made use of natural bends or features in the wood, especially for the animal figure-head. It took him a month to do the job, more or less single-handed, which compares well with the three weeks needed by Henry Ainalik, master umiak builder, and two helpers to build a slightly larger Eskimo umiak at Ivugivik in Hudson's Bay. They had been asked to do this by the National Museum of Canada so that the museum could have one before the traditional art of making them died out. The umiak's hull covering was made from the skins of seven bearded seals which had been buried in the sand of the beach for a month to prepare them by making the hair easily removable.

The launching of Johnsen's cowhide boat took place on July 2nd 1971. It was carried down the slipway by a crew of six students from the Oslo University Bårum Rowing Club, to the applause of a considerable watching crowd. Rather to their surprise it neither sank nor turned over, but floated gracefully and steadily. Soon the students were aboard and off for a trial run with the paddles, which had been hewn from single pieces of timber to match the shape of those in the rock carvings at Kalnes on which the boat had been based. The shipyard workers on the big tanker across the river stopped their riveting for a moment, waved their tin hats and cheered. Soon the vessel with its silky hair-covered hull was moving up the branch of the river which runs right through the middle of the town of Frederikstad. Bicyclists stopped to stare in astonishment, and one lady even dropped her shopping bag as the strange but elegant craft with its animal head and double bow rode easily by.

Tests on the following days showed that this craft was no fantasy. The double bow worked extremely well, especially when beaching. The crew just went on paddling until the under section of the double bow touched shore, lifted, slowed and stopped. The paddlers then jumped out and carried it effortlessly up the beach. In fact, one of the most interesting things was that it was very much easier making a Bronze Age type landing like this on an open beach, or rocks, than coming alongside a modern jetty or pier, when the high bow always seemed to get entangled in any mooring rope, or caught under the timbers of the pier. The craft rode well, took a load of three-quarters of a ton without any bother, and generally was very handy. Kneeling on their life-jackets, the students found

OPPOSITE
The replica ready
for its tests.

that they could comfortably keep up a steady speed of two and a half knots over a measured kilometre paddled both ways to cancel out winds and currents.

During the tests, southern Norway remained in the centre of a glorious anti-cyclone, and Oslo was the hottest capital in Europe, so rough seas were hard to come by. The best that could be done was to circle the craft with a speedboat going at maximum revolutions. It was clear even from this that the skin craft was a good sea boat, rode abrupt waves lightly and easily, and took very little spray aboard.

Of course this experiment does not absolutely prove that the Scandinavian rock carvings do represent skin boats. But it does show that it was possible to build such a craft with the materials easily available to Bronze Age man, and that it had the effectiveness at sea which one would expect from the predecessors of the Vikings.

8

The Ferriby Boats: Blue Clay on the Humber

Ted Wright is a Yorkshire businessman. He has always taught his children to keep a sharp eye on the ground they are walking over, because that is the way to find fossils, small flint tools and so on. He has good reason to encourage them to do this, because he has always done it himself and in his case it has given him a rare distinction. He is one of the few men in Europe to have found a Bronze Age boat.

In the early 1930s a change in the currents of the River Humber in the north of England stripped away a thick blanket of recent silt and revealed on the foreshore at North Ferriby, some seven miles upstream from Hull, the surface of a bed of blue clay overlaying peat. This same surface had been visible back in the 1880s and was uncovered again off and on in the 1930s. After that, it appeared intermittently until the late 1950s, and briefly again after the severe winter of 1963. It is now thickly covered, but presumably is always likely to show up again at short notice when some quirk of the current starts moving the usual silt covering.

This occasionally-visible bed of blue clay attracted considerable interest in the thirties from geologists and botanists, especially the latter, because of the well-known preservative element in peat, which does not support the fungi and bacteria that cause decay in wood and plant remains. Ted Wright and his brother were among the younger collectors working on the riverbank, extending their usual interest in fossils and flint tools to the early botanical remains. The keen watch they kept on this layer as it was regularly scoured by the tides was further rewarded by the finding of various objects of wood and stone that seemed once to have been used or made by prehistoric man. But in the early spring of 1938 they saw something of a very different kind. Ted was walking along on the seaward side of the mud, while his brother was searching a parallel but more inland stretch, when he saw sticking out of the blue clay and silt the ends of three planks.

'Hey, Willie,' he called out. 'I've found a Viking ship.'

A ship it was, but not a Viking one.

They then set about checking what distance the planks ran under the mud, by prodding along them with a walking stick. As far as could be told, they seemed to stretch about forty feet (twelve metres) at a depth of three feet (91 cms) or so, and to be fastened together with pegs. In due course Ted Wright was able to organise some trial excavations, but conditions were always difficult. The remains of the vessel were nearer the low-water mark than the high, the mud was sticky, and they never had more than five hours to dig and refill their trial trenches between tides. On one occasion he and his brother had the help of four other people, which allowed them to clear a considerable section across the middle. Any small finds apart from the planks were also carefully kept; they included some reeds, halves of acorns and hazel nuts, two shells of small crabs and a lump of white flint.

It was now becoming clear that the vessel from which these had come was neither Viking nor pegged, but of a unique kind. Its basic parts consisted of a very large, strong, and flat keel-plank in two pieces scarfed or joined together with an overlap of some three inches, to which was attached on each side a rather thinner plank. These fitted into a groove in the edge of the keel-plank and were fastened to it by very cunning stitching of cracked yew branches in the thickness of the wood, which also ran over battens covering the joins. Across the three planks ran a number of cross-bars which fitted into slots in cleats. These cleats had been left standing above the thickness of the planks when the original shipwrights had adzed them out. These wood-workers had also used the original thickness of the wood to leave a rather intriguing upward bend at the only well-preserved end of the keel-plank. The seams between the planks were filled with moss and in two places cracks in the planks had been carefully repaired.

OPPOSITE
Boat No. 1 in 1946, on the day C. W. Phillips decided to help with total recovery. Notice the line of holes and stitching on the right and behind them the cross-bar running under the cleats

The Wrights had hoped to organise a full-scale excavation and salvage operation for 1940 before any of the craft was washed away, but unfortunately by now the war was imminent and little more could be done. So the three pieces which looked most likely to be washed away were lifted and taken to what was to be their wartime

home, under the staging of an old greenhouse in Ted Wright's family home. Being pretty damp, the greenhouse did not do at all badly as a storehouse.

In late 1940 Ted Wright came home for a week's leave, and he went to see how the blue-clay band was getting on. Once again he was in luck; this time he found a second boat, though it had only the centre plank surviving. He managed single-handed to clear each end of it and, on a subsequent leave, a stretch across the middle. This confirmed that it was of the same general type as the first boat.

Three more sections of exposed planks which might otherwise have been lost were also lifted on these occasions. Unfortunately this time they were stored, not in Ted Wright's greenhouse, but in the Hull Museum, which was set on fire by incendiary bombs during an air raid in 1942 and burnt down. Natural forces, too, did their share. Sometime between 1941 and the end of the war some three feet of the seaward end of the second boat was carried away by the current and lost, and the first boat also suffered some damage.

However, most of what was lost had already been recorded, so the erosion of the bank was not as much a set-back as it might

Part of the timbers of Boat No. 1 in 1946, showing one of the yew stitches and the moss caulking in between the planks.

otherwise have been. By 1946 Ted Wright was a civilian again and in a position to try and do something about the two-thirds of Boat No. 1 and the major part of Boat No. 2's centre plank that remained. While continuing to record as much detail as possible, he endeavoured to find some organisation which would take on the proper salvaging of the whole of the remains. This was all the more urgent because it was generally felt that one more bad winter could well wash them away—and indeed the ice-floes of the winter of 1946–7, which was to become notorious for its long cold spell, might well have done this.

Luckily, while they were doing the best they could do with only a few helpers to extract small pieces which showed the principal points of construction, they were visited by C. W. Phillips, one of the heroes of the Sutton Hoo excavation described in Chapter 9. Ted Wright, with considerable cunning, had reserved a very interesting piece for clearing during C. W. Phillips's visit; it was where the end of the first strake of Boat No. 1's side fitted into the central keel-plank, a very crucial part of the construction. When they had done all the clearing they could during that particular low tide and were beginning to record what they had exposed, Ted Wright remembers C. W. Phillips sitting on the edge of the hole in the mud and saying 'Something must be done'. And something was done. The interest of the British Museum, the National Maritime Museum and the Royal Navy was aroused and at last, eight years and one world war after the original find, a major rescue operation was organised for the autumn.

The tides, the weather, and the state of the silt all looked promising. The plan was to have a group of archaeologists clear the two boats, then slide under them a sledge made from a thin boiler plate, suitably reinforced, and then haul the lot by power winch up the muddy bank to the side of the river.

The operation began on October 23rd. Even in reasonable conditions, it would not have been the easiest of work. Each tide refilled the boats with silt, which had to be re-cleared every time before excavation could continue. Though firm at first, the mud soon became puddled and gluey when trodden on, and by the end of a low-tide period, every step was a dragging effort. A cofferdam, like the Roskilde one, would have solved many problems, but the expense of it at that period just after the war put it out of the question. So the sledge it had to be.

The tide was only low in daylight for about a fortnight, so they had the pressure of that behind them as well as the threat of winter. Finding the right place for the tractor with the winch on it was another problem. But eventually everything was ready and the power was applied to the hauling line. It should have been a dramatic moment as the boiler-plate sledge started cutting into the mud under Boat No. 1. Instead, the two-inch (five-cm) steel wire broke, broke again, and then again. Finally, after it had parted five times, they substituted a three-and-a-half-inch (nine-cm) trawler warp. At last it seemed that the scheme was going to work. Slowly the front edge sliced through the thick gluey clay under the ancient timbers. But then, when it was about half-way along the length of the keel, something much more sinister than any snapping of wires started to happen. The friction increased, the clay underneath the vessel started to pile up and that in turn started to crumple the precious wood of the craft, which by now was widely agreed to be unique and to date back at least to the pre-Roman Iron Age. The feelings of the excavators can be imagined. The tide was turning and there was not much daylight left. On top of everything else, the wind was rising and there was a serious danger that if a storm blew up at high tide, the now thoroughly loosened boat might be washed away completely, or disintegrate. It was a moment for emergency action. The excavators decided to dismantle all the parts of the boat that were not already on the sledge and carry them up the bank. Then the front of the boiler-plate was cleared, and the prow of the sledge fitted on. By this time the lower part was already awash in the rising water. With continuous adjustments they heaved away as darkness fell, narrowly racing the tide to the high-water mark.

The next morning they hurried back to the site again, just beating various souvenir-hunters by a short head, and completed the collection of any remaining small pieces. Boat No. 1 was now ready for full recording and storage.

With Boat No. 2, now that they knew the sledge idea was imprac-tical, they were less ambitious. They waited until the tides were suitable again, sawed the single central plank into a number of lengths and carried them up the bank; the largest piece needed no fewer than eight men to take its weight.

The thick rescued pieces were then all carefully packed in shavings and sent off to the National Maritime Museum at Greenwich by lorry. There the slow process of preserving them in glycerine was due to begin, but once again the aftermath of war took its toll.

OPPOSITE
Boat No. 2 cleared for recording in 1946.

There were neither suitable tanks, buildings nor much money available and the pieces of the two boats had to spend that very hard winter lying on the ground outside covered with sacking. The polycthylene glycol method, used so successfully on the Roskilde ships, was not to be evolved until 1959. When eventually the pieces did get into the glycerine, shortage of staff meant a continual struggle to carry out the various checks and whatever changes of the solution became necessary. Finally the unequal battle had to be given up when, amongst other things, the smell became so intolerable that visitors to the Museum were affected. So, in Ted Wright's own words, though Boat No. 2 was stabilised, Boat No. 1 was an almost total write-off.

One would have thought that the Ferriby story had already had more than enough drama in it, but it was still not finished. In 1963, Ted Wright returned from a trip to India and the East where he had seen some of the 'sewn' boats that are still made and used in places with their planks fastened entirely by lashings, not nails or rivets. Doubtless, as he says, stimulated by this and the fact that the blue clay had once more had another of its irregular clearings of silt, he persuaded his family to go for a walk one blowy Sunday afternoon and have another look at the site which had once seen such tense efforts. 'As usual when they got there it was 'eyes down', and he and his son walked practically straight up to the parts of a boat of the now familiar Ferriby type. Sticking up out of the mud were some bits of planks clearly showing the ends of broken stitches. At first they thought this might be more of Boat No. 1 but in fact it turned out to be nearly a thirty-foot (nine-metre) length of yet a third boat, with two of its bottom planks surviving.

This time the archaeological side of the excavation was directed by Ted Wright himself, while John Bartlett, the then Director of the Hull Museum, who was on the site within three-quarters of an hour of hearing the news of the new find, was in charge of the lifting. At first they planned to take it up piece by piece, but in the end persuaded themselves to attempt the far more ambitious task of lifting the vessel whole. The plan was to build a cradle of scaffolding and plywood round the vessel, drag this up the bank, and then lift it onto a lorry by crane. Unfortunately the plywood cradle inside the scaffolding was not properly secured and the vessel broke up during the last stages of the lift. Nevertheless, all the wood was recovered and taken to one of the Hull Museum's workshops where it is currently being treated by soaking in carbowax, a form of polyethylene glycol.

To compensate for all the physical disasters of time and circumstance which have dogged the Ferriby boats, there is the consolation of the meticulous recording which Ted Wright has done throughout. This at least enables us to get a very thorough idea of what did remain of these craft. This is all the more important because radio-carbon tests on various pieces have now shown that they are not Iron Age at all, but date back much earlier to the Bronze Age. In fact a bronze knife and some pottery found near the boats would not clash with the radio-carbon dates which suggest that the three vessels were built, used and finally dismantled when too old somewhere between 1500 BC and 750 BC.

One of the many curious points about these vessels is that they do have some parallels of a sort, but the closest one is a good deal later. This is what is known as the 'Brigg raft', a strange vessel which was excavated in 1880 in a brickyard by the River Ancholme, a tributary of the Humber which enters it at South Ferriby. What the nineteenth-century excavators recorded then was a large craft with squared-off ends and ten crossbars running over the five stitched-together planks of its flat bottom. These crossbars fitted into slots in cleats just as in the Ferriby boats.

There was also a dug-out found at Brigg in 1884. This had a repair on it which was secured by a bar running through cleats, thus putting it to some extent in the Ferriby school of construction. Unfortunately this great dug-out was also destroyed by the wartime burning-down of the Hull Museum.

So it seems that in this part of Yorkshire in the Bronze Age from 1500 BC on, a specialised school of boat-building existed. Another of its characteristics, besides the cross-bars in cleats, the stitching and the battens over the joins, was the moss used for caulking. It is a type only found in woodlands, but although a very large amount of it must have been needed in these fifty-foot craft, the builders obviously found it had the particular qualities they needed, because only in one very short stretch of caulking did they use as an alternative the common hair-moss.

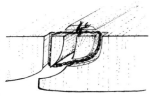

The 'secret stitching' technique. The cracked yew branches were protected within the thickness of the planking.

Then there is what Ted Wright has aptly called the 'secret-stitching' technique. This uses holes sunk into the thickness of the wood so that the stitching of thin yew branches, twisted and cracked for flexibility, was never in danger of being scuffed or torn when the boat was dragged ashore. The technique is virtually

A suggested recon-
struction of the
Ferriby windlass.

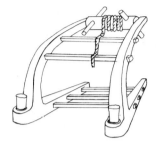

identical to that used on the Cheops ship. The battens which cover
the joins of the planks also recall Maori practice in the Pacific.
This does not mean, as some optimists might be inclined to suggest,
that there was contact between prehistoric Britain and Egypt or even
New Zealand—only that at the same technological stage, men often
tended to produce the same technological solution to problems,
wherever they might be.

Finally there is the way the wood was not bent but carved out
of the mass. This meant that at the point where the lowest side strake
curved round and joined the side of the bent-up end of the keel-
plank, the original wood-worker had to achieve a double curve in
three dimensions—a very considerable achievement.

Besides these details of technique which were clearly visible,
there are a number of puzzles. There is, for instance, a cleat under
the bow. Was this to hold in place a lashing which went round the
planks of the bows and held them together? Or was it one point of
attachment for hauling this very heavy craft up on the shore?
There was a V-shaped piece of timber found near the boats in
1939 and destroyed in the war, which had one curved arm and one
straight arm with three holes in it, of which the outside one still
held the remains of a peg. By comparison with modern examples
still in use on the coasts of Finland, Ted Wright has interpreted
this as possibly the side piece of a portable windlass. This might
well support the hauling-up theory. Then there are some shallow
furrows running fore-and-aft under the bows. In Maori canoe-
building practice, rather similar ones are used to reduce the drag of
the craft through the water. Was this the function of the Ferriby
grooves? There are also various apparently unused cleats on the
bottom of the inside of the boat. Were they to hold supports for
thwarts on which paddlers sat, or could they be part of some
primitive form of mast step? The former seems more likely.

Finally, there is perhaps the biggest question of all. What were
the ends like? No trace of them was found by the excavators. In his
first reconstruction of what a Ferriby boat might originally have
looked like, Ted Wright suggested a rather punt-like craft with
flat gunwhales. This would make these craft definitely river boats,
ferries perhaps for taking people, cattle and goods up and down and
across the Humber.

More recently he has put forward another interpretation with
a high bow and stern. This would make the Ferriby vessels much
more likely to be sea-going types. There are three good reasons

OPPOSITE
Above The recon-
structed Oseberg ship
in the Viking Ship
Museum in Oslo.
Below Towing the
Bronze Age replica
out to sea for its tests.
Despite the speed of
the tow, it rides the
waves so well that the
crew of students are
quite unconcerned.

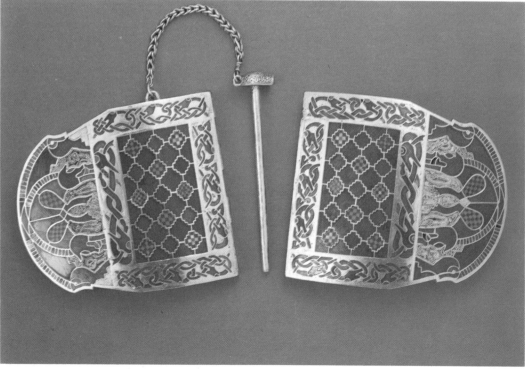

why this second interpretation may be right. First of all, there are still in existence some very interesting Portuguese fishing boats called *saveiros* and *meia luas*, which have high bows and sterns. Although very effective for fishing off beaches into the open Atlantic, these craft are so primitive in design that they have neither keel, rudder, mast, nor ribs. On the other hand, they do have flat bottoms attached by cross members, though these do not run through cleats. This has suggested to some people that their basic design may go back a long way, possibly even as far as the Bronze Age.

Then there are some coins from the Atlantic area, some Gaulish of about 100 BC and a late Romano-British one, which show simple high-ended craft quite unlike the normal Roman variety.

Finally there is the evidence of classical literature. Julius Caesar fought a great sea-battle off Brittany with a famous sea-going tribe of the Gauls called the Venetii and was so surprised by the unusual nature of their ships that he left a very detailed description of them. They had leather sails, iron chains to their anchors, oak planks caulked with seaweed, flat bottoms secured with massive cross members, and high bows and sterns. The use of oak, seaweed caulking instead of mortices and tenons, and flat bottoms was particularly different to Roman practice.

All this suggests there may have been up the west coast of Europe in the pre-Roman period a tradition of tough, simple ship-building with flat bottoms fastened by cross-members and high bows and sterns, which spilled over during the Bronze Age into the Humber to produce something more elaborate than dug-outs or skin boats. There is some archaeological evidence, too, to back up this idea of a western European tradition which was different from either that of the classical Greek and Roman world, or the northern craft of the Vikings' predecessors.

One of the first Roman ships ever to be properly excavated and recorded was found back in 1910, not in the Mediterranean as one might expect, but in Edwardian London on the south bank of the River Thames. It was spotted by two members of the London County Council during the digging of the foundations for County Hall; they noticed a dark curving line under some fourteen feet (4·27 metres) of silt. The contractor involved was at once ordered to proceed with great care and this resulted in due course in the finding of part of the bottom and side of a Roman ship. Much less was known then about the technique of Roman ship construction,

Above The great gold buckle from the Sutton Hoo burial chamber.
Below One of the garnet-inlaid gold shoulder clasps.

97

G

but there was no question about the date of this particular ship because a number of Roman coins were found with it, two actually being stuck beneath its ribs, as well as a quantity of pottery and parts of some Roman leather shoes. Even if this perhaps seventy-foot-long (21·3-metre) Roman coaster was neither as impressive or as complete as the Gokstad ship, the then director of the London Museum took a tip from the Oslo Ship Museum when the County Hall vessel was presented to him. The Roman remains were packed in a huge box forty feet long, weighing ten tons, which was placed on two trucks hauled by no fewer than twelve horses. The procession set out on its journey from the County Hall site to the then home of the London Museum in Kensington Palace at 4 a.m. in the morning, led by the Museum director on horseback. Even so, it took all day for its journey, and like the Gokstad ship had done in Oslo, created a great traffic jam. But the Museum director took very good care to extract the maximum publicity from the situation. On the tarpaulin covering the box, he had made sure there was stencilled in large white letters 'Roman Boat—London Museum'! Unfortunately this craft was so incomplete that no attempt was made to reconstruct it then, though there is a chance that this may be done, now so much more is known about early ships.

Subsequent finds, as we have seen, have shown that this craft's mortice-and-tenon-joined strakes and shell construction with the ribs inserted later were characteristically Roman. Even so, it was made of oak grown probably in Gaul, a non-Roman practice, and the excavators' cautious hint of a local tradition of ship-building when they called it a 'ship of the Roman period' rather than a 'Roman ship', was to be more than justified in 1962.

In that year, the construction of a new riverside embankment on the north side of the Thames had reached Blackfriars when a mechanical grab struck some massive black oak timbers in the bed of the river. Peter Marsden of the Guildhall Museum was on the site the same day and at once organised rescue operations, in which, among others, members of the neighbouring Mermaid Theatre were enthusiastic helpers in between rehearsals. In a situation that would have been familiar to the Ferriby excavators, and anticipated those of the *Amsterdam* (cf. Chapter 10), the remains of the Blackfriars wreck lay under the bed of the river which, though covered by twenty feet (six metres) of water at high tide, was clear for about two hours at low water. Just as at Ferriby in 1947, the excavation was planned for the October spring tides. The

Peter Marsden excavating the Roman ship at Blackfriars from the muddy bottom of the River Thames.

mechanical excavator responsible for the original find was lent to dig down to the wreck, and the London Fire Brigade volunteered to pump out the water. By the second day, they had found the side of the craft and they could feel the ribs underfoot, but in making the hole the excavator had churned so much mud into the water that the pump kept getting blocked and could not suck it out. Recording by touch, not sight, was therefore necessary, but the

99

difficulties of doing the measuring for this survey by feeling beneath a thick broth of muddy water were intense. So in November, with three further low tides, a different method was tried. This time the mechanical excavator dug down to the level of the wreck, then moved to one side to make an even deeper hole which acted as a sump. Into this the archaeologists and their helpers washed the mud and gravel off the timbers by a water jet. In this way, they were able to clear and record a considerable part of the wreck.

Then they had a stroke of luck. The line of the cofferdam which was enabling the new embankment to be built was found to cross one half of the wreck, and so they were given yet another three days in July 1963. Though this made it simple for them to date the ship, because they found that the gravel over this different part was full of Roman pottery, they had to spend most of the permitted extra time removing this gravel overburden. It looked as though once again the job would be incomplete. But just as at Ferriby the luck had always seemed to run against the excavators, here it was the other way round. The Lord Mayor was due to visit the site, but could not come until three days after they were supposed to finish; so once more the magic number of three extra days was granted. Then, after the Lord Mayor's visit, a national newspaper started a campaign to save the ship, and literally one hour before it was due to be destroyed, it was decided that the timbers should be lifted and taken to the Guildhall Museum.

As a result it was possible to study properly the unique nature of this ship. It was a small Roman vessel, some fifty-five feet (16·7 metres) long, but the remarkable thing about it was that it was not built in the normal Roman fashion at all. The strakes were not joined by mortices and tenons but had been nailed to massive floor timbers, and the seams were caulked with hazel twigs. It had no keel and a nearly flat bottom, which the sides met at a fairly sharp angle. Like the County Hall vessel, it was also made of oak.

So was yet another Roman vessel, which by good luck Peter Marsden had caught a glimpse of in 1959 during the building of the New Guy's Hospital surgical wing in London, even though it could not be excavated. The building's foundation trenches only revealed part of this craft, but there was enough to show that it was a small flat-bottomed river barge which had been abandoned in a creek off the River Thames in about the second century AD. Its significance was greatly increased by the subsequent finding of the much larger and more complete Blackfriars ship, because of the similarity of the way the two craft were built. The New Guy's Hospital boat also had nailed strakes, not joined by mortices and tenons, with hazel-twig caulking in its place. Although not properly excavated, enough was found to say that though it was a different form of vessel, it was still built in the same way as the Blackfriars ship; so it seems certain that there was a local tradition of ship-building in Britain during the Roman period which produced vessels by quite different methods and with quite different details to the Roman ones.

But there still remains exactly the same query about these three London ships as the Ferriby ones. The ends of all the bows and sterns have disappeared and not been found. If those of the London ships were high, then it is possible that they derived ultimately from whatever Atlantic tradition may have produced the Ferriby craft, those of the Venetii, and the ships on the Gaulish and Roman coins. There are also a number of Roman and other period wrecks which have recently been found in Holland, Switzerland and Germany. They seem to be large flat-bottomed river barges, have L-shaped junctions between bottom and sides, have nail-fastened planks with caulking in between and be derived originally from a split dug-out technique—that is to say, roughly speaking, a dug-out is split in half and the two halves separated with a flat bottom. This type of craft may also have led up to the 'cog', the flat-bottomed high-sided trader of medieval times, as opposed to the much more curved, probably rounder-bottomed 'hulk'. A good example of the 'hulk' can be seen carved on the font of Winchester Cathedral and on the early seals of a number of towns like New Shoreham. It may in turn be derived from the rounder-bottomed river craft of the Romans, which were used frequently to carry great loads of wine casks up and down the French rivers. What, if any, the exact relationship between all these different types was, only further study and finds will tell.

It is a complicated picture—but then that is usually nearer to the historical truth than an over-simplified one. What is certain is that the rafts, skin-boats and dug-outs of the earliest European sea travellers must have gone through many varied forms before they became Ferriby and Romano-British types, let alone Viking longships, 'cogs' and 'hulks'; but it will probably be many years, if ever, before we understand exactly how it all happened.

Drawing of a twelfth-century carving of a 'hulk' in Winchester Cathedral.

9

Sutton Hoo: the Million Pound Grave

1938 was a rather slack year on the estate of Mrs Edith Pretty, JP, at Sutton Hoo, across the River Deben from the little town of Woodbridge in Suffolk. So she decided to investigate a group of barrows which stood on the heathland of a small promontory above the estuary and were part of the estate. These mounds were known locally as Sutton Hills or Little Egypt because of their dryness and dustiness.

After some consultation with the Ipswich Museum, the excavation was put into the hands of Basil Brown. He was the son of a local farmer who had developed a great knowledge of local soils and an extraordinary flair for finding antiquities. Eventually he had became a part-time employee of the Ipswich Museum. Mrs Pretty gave him lodgings in an upstairs room in her chauffeur's cottage and agreed to pay him thirty shillings a week to take charge of the excavations.

Mrs Pretty herself may have been tempted to start on the largest mound, but Basil Brown very sensibly preferred to try his hand on some of the smaller ones. The three he dug that year all proved different. One mound had a cremated burial intact in it, the next had been ransacked, while the third held an unburnt body. The contents of all three, however—fragments of weapons, blue glass, bowls and ornaments—proved that the mounds were not Bronze Age in date, as might have been expected, but Anglo-Saxon. Furthermore, there was one additional find that was to prove very significant. Basil Brown put a trench into the round third mound from east to west, and very soon came across a heap of clenched nails which had once fastened together the clinker planking of a boat. There were some forty of these in all, of which seven had been left in their original position by the grave robbers of later times. These seven showed clearly that the original burial in the mound had been in a boat.

Mrs Pretty was sufficiently encouraged by all this to go ahead again the following year. Basil Brown was duly summoned and walked down to the mounds with Mrs Pretty. 'Which would you like excavated, madam?' he asked. 'What about that one?' was the answer. 'That one' was apparently the biggest, some nine feet (2·74 metres) high and over a hundred feet (30·5 metres) long. Guided by his experience the previous year, Basil Brown thought there might be a boat there too, so he put in his trench from the east along the original axis of the mound, gradually working down to the old ground-surface level. One of Basil Brown's assistants was Jack Jacobs, Mrs Pretty's gardener, a willing helper but one with not much experience of archaeology, and it was he who at midday on May 11th 1939, made the crucial first find—one rivet, and then another, and another, forming a line. He was about to pick them up when Basil Brown saw what was happening out of the corner of his eye. He rushed across and pushed Jacobs aside just in time to stop him lifting anything. Basil Brown then carefully cleared the line of rivets down with trowel and bare hands. What he was expecting was the bow of a small boat, something like the previous year's find. But the rivets went on and on and down and down, steadily widening apart. Very soon it was clear that whatever he had found was very large indeed.

It was impossible to keep all knowledge of such a remarkable find completely quiet, and in June rumours that enquiries about Viking ship burials were being made reached the ears of C. W. Phillips, Fellow of Selwyn College, Cambridge, and secretary of the Pre-historic Society. In due course he arranged a visit to the Sutton Hoo mound which had been the source of these rumours. Round the heap of sand that had been excavated he walked and there before him was an astonishing sight, one never seen in Britain before —the remains of a large ship nearly a hundred feet (30·5 metres) long and many centuries old. Within an hour the British Museum and the Ministry of Works had been informed, and not so long after that C. W. Phillips was asked to take charge of the excavation.

As he said himself, he was flabbergasted, because he did not quite see how anybody was going to take it on; but since nobody in England knew anything about the technique anyway, it seemed to him that he might as well have a bash. So, in his own words, bash he did.

The manner of the excavation had been decided by Basil Brown's clearing-down to the level of the ship. The only thing now was to continue on the same lines, in contrast to the Swedes who had excavated a number of Viking ship mounds by cutting a succession of vertical sections across them. This had a number of advantages, like doing away with any risk of the sides slipping in, but it never provided the splendid overall panoramic view of the craft itself, which was to be such a distinguishing feature of Sutton Hoo.

At this early stage Basil Brown had worked up to the edge of what might be a burial chamber and the immediate question was how much remained of any burial which might have been placed in the ship. As many of the other mounds on the estate showed signs of having been robbed, as well as the ones excavated in 1938, the excavators were not very optimistic. But on Sunday, July 22nd, the tantalising promise of the bits of wood, iron and bronze sticking out of the central part of the ship suddenly crystallised in a way no one had expected. The trowelling and brushing of the sand suddenly revealed a jewel made of garnets and gold. This find did two things. It finally confirmed that the craft was Anglo-Saxon, not Viking, and it made clear that the excavators were involved in an exceptional situation. C. W. Phillips was away in Woodbridge and when he came back and saw what had been found, one of the excavators remembers that his first comment was 'Oh, my godfathers!' and the rest of the day he went round saying to himself over and over again, 'Oh dear, oh dear!'

More pieces of jewellery now began to appear in quick succession all over the area where what had evidently been a burial chamber had collapsed in the centre of the ship. These gave the excavators the experience, rare in archaeology, of finding gold, of clearing away the sand and coming on an object still as bright and shining as when it had been put there more than 1,300 years before. Then a number of coins appeared, but unfortunately they did not, as was first hoped, solve the problem of the exact date of the ship. The dating of the coins by the style and metallurgical analysis turned out to be a matter of extreme complication. Broadly speaking, they are thought now to have been collected together between AD 625 and 630, and an interesting suggestion is that the forty coins were the wages of the oarsmen who were to take the king, or whoever was the owner of the treasure, on his last voyage.

Cleaning the sand
from the contents of
the burial chamber.
In the right
foreground is the great
silver Byzantine dish.

Over the next few days many remarkable objects were found, some in an extreme state of decay, requiring very delicate lifting. The helmet, the shield, the iron stand, the stone bar, the cauldron, dishes, bowls, weapons, and the lyre were among the grave-goods which all together made up the richest treasure ever dug from British soil and which is now on display in the British Museum in London. With the pressure of this flow of extraordinary finds bearing down on them, the tension amongst the excavators would have been strong enough anyway. The imminence of the war heightened it further. Everyone had his own *War of the Worlds* fantasy of mass bombing raids wiping out the site, yet these were hardly more fantastic than what was actually happening. Professor Stuart Piggott of Edinburgh University remembers vividly the moment when they lifted and turned over a big silver dish, and there on its back was the control mark of the Byzantine Emperor Anastasius I— the name 'Anastasius', clearly readable, proclaiming that this great piece of silverwork lying on the Suffolk grass had come all the way there thirteen centuries ago from Byzantium.

The facilities available for this, the richest excavation ever carried out in Britain, were almost ludicrous. They amounted to a few scaffold poles and some tarpaulins, two policemen to keep an eye on things, and the thick damp moss growing in the copse nearby. All the finds, which with very great generosity were given to the nation by Mrs Pretty, went up to the British Museum carefully covered in this soft dark moss. As a wrapping, it could scarcely have been bettered.

When everything finally had been lifted, the excavators were left with one thing missing and one thing very much present. The absentee was the body of some seventh-century East Anglian king, or whoever else had been honoured by the burial. Still remaining was what was left of the ship itself.

C. W. Phillips once described how he himself worked at revealing the hull. The actual ribs and planks had completely disintegrated, but where they had once been they had left the sand a different colour, and the rivets and their roves or plates over which the rivet-ends bent still survived as rusty lumps. So standing in the ship he worked outward with his trowel towards where the skin of the boat had once been, slicing the sand down carefully. What first appeared were pink patches, and these were the warning rust signs that a rivet was about to appear. In this way, he established the pattern of the rivets, and the planking they had once secured.

The ghost of the great open rowing boat that eventually appeared was some eighty feet (twenty-four metres) long without bow and stern, fourteen feet (4·27 metres) at its widest, drawing about two feet (sixty-one cms). Clinker-built, it had nine one-inch (2·5-cm) thick planks of oak each side, scarfed together in varying lengths, and twenty-six ribs. Along the gunwhales had been hook-shaped tholes for the oars, and a strengthened side-section for the steering-oar. Obviously, it was already an old ship when it had been hauled up the hillside and lowered into its sandy grave, because it had had a number of repairs made to it.

Possibly the most difficult question about it is whether it had a mast or not. No signs of the necessary fittings have ever been found, and its keel hardly has the depth to give convincing evidence on this point. So maybe it was the last or so of a long tradition of great rowing vessels in the north which wound their way through the complicated shoals of the North Sea in the period just before the

Basil Brown standing by the Sutton Hoo ship mound before the re-excavation started in 1965.

striped sails of the Vikings introduced new proportions both of piracy and lengthy sea travel.

The ship itself was the only thing that could not be sent off to the British Museum, wrapped in moss or otherwise. It was a mere impression in the sand, and nothing could then be done with it. So with the war starting, the great trench through the mound was filled with bracken and left. And so quickly was it forgotten, under the impact of greater events, that it was not so long afterwards that this convenient dip in the ground was being used as a useful feature in an armoured-vehicle training course. Not until twenty-six years later did archaeologists, rather than tank commanders, return in purposeful force to the site.

The second stage of the excavation of the Sutton Hoo ship took place between 1965 and 1967. By then the dust of war had settled—quite literally in the case of the trench through the mound; archaeological techniques had advanced, and it was thought a good idea to re-excavate the site, under the direction this time of R. L. S. Bruce-Mitford, in order to clear up both some old problems and some new ones which had appeared with lengthy study of the finds.

It soon became clear that it was well worthwhile. Careful sifting of the original spoil from the burial chamber produced small additional pieces of the helmet, the shield, and the standard, part of a bucket handle, and a third boar's head decoration that had been missing from the large hanging bowl. A survey of the whole site also increased the number of known mounds from eleven to sixteen. When cleared again, the ghost ship was still a very impressive sight, though the top two or three strakes on each side had gone, and part of one side towards the stern had split and bulged inwards. Another unusual find, a retrospective tribute to the recent role of the mound, was a four-inch mortar smoke-canister in the wartime weapon pit which had also helped to destroy the stern.

The ship itself now presented an unusual problem: should it be preserved, or should it be destroyed? The answer might seem obvious. But in fact, after much thought, the Ancient Monuments Board decided on destruction, and for good reasons. To start with, the task of preserving a ship seventy-six feet (twenty-three metres) long which consisted only of two thousand rusty bolts and some

This drawing by Alan Sorrell shows how the Sutton Hoo ship might have been hauled to its final resting place. The trench awaits it at the top of the hill.

BBC Copyright

stains in the sand was a very difficult one. Furthermore, a good deal of information was still waiting to be found, but only at the expense of the ghost ship in the sand. Was there, for instance, a sacrifice under the ship, as sometimes happened in Viking ship burials? Or could the oars be there? In the event, neither of these appeared, but the archaeologists were able to establish the precise angles the bolts had been set at, and by cutting several sections through the keel they really found out its shape properly.

But before the destruction took place in order to acquire this additional information, every means was used to achieve as detailed an account as possible of the ship. Besides the usual photographic and drawing techniques, a three dimensional record of the position and angle of every single rivet was made. Above all, it was decided to undertake an operation then unique in British archaeology—the making of a cast of the entire inside of the hull. Besides using six and a half tons of plaster to cover the remaining seventy-six-foot-long shape, this operation presented all sorts of unknown and complicated problems. The mould was to be of plaster of Paris, both because it was cheap enough for the huge quantities required, and also because it set quickly. Before the actual moulding started, a mock-up of part of the ship was made, using excavated sand from the mound and with flints standing in for the rusty rivets.

On this they first tried applying the plaster of Paris directly to the sand, but the result was disaster. When the plaster had set and was lifted, it brought away with it not only the top layer of sand but the imitation rivets as well. In the second and third attempts, a hardener was applied to the sand first, and when it had set, a mixture of tallow and oil was put on that. The result was failure again. The sand still came up with the plaster.

For the fourth attempt, a layer of polythene was put over a section of the ship with little slits cut in a cross to go over each rivet. These in turn were protected by their own small square of polythene covered with modelling clay to make a sort of 'oyster'. This worked much better. The rivets and the surface of the ship stayed in place when the plaster was lifted, but the technique was not quite satisfactory because there were so many wrinkles in the polythene that the true shape of the vessel did not appear on the mould.

Finally, at the fifth attempt, the persistence of the technicians from the British Museum Research Laboratory, led by Peter van Geersdaele, was rewarded. Paper towelling was soaked in water and laid as flatly as possible on the surface of the ship. Again, gaps were left for the protective 'oysters' over each rivet. The towelling was worked down as smooth as possible by paint-brushes, being sprayed all the time by a garden hose to keep it wet and clinging. Then polythene tubes filled with sand were placed to mark out the area of each section and the wet plaster poured in. The team had just eight minutes to do this before the plaster set, and in the process they had to reinforce the plaster with scrim and put in lifting handles of bent gas-piping. The edges of each section were cut to a slope to overlap and hold the previous section in position, and also treated with French polish and rape oil. When the whole ship had been covered with this thick white covering, in tight-fitting sections, including the ribs with their difficult raised shape, the lifting could then begin.

This was always a dramatic moment. It was done either by man-power, or a pulley attached to the embedded lifting handles. At first there would be no movement in answer to the heaving. Then the effort would tell, the section would start to move, and up it would come, tatters of the paper towelling flapping in the breeze from its underside. Then there would be a hasty look to see that the rivets and ship stain in the sand were untouched, and the sections would be carried off and carefully loaded onto a lorry for transport to the British Museum workshops. In all eighty-five sections were needed, and the operation took three weeks to make a permanent record of the shape Basil Brown had come upon in the mound.

Back at the workshops these sections were eventually set up, upside down, on timber supports and oil drums, for a complete cast to be made from them. The joins were filled in where necessary, any wrinkles removed, and where the rivet 'oysters' had been, a clay filling with a hole in it to represent the rivet was placed. The whole mould was then covered with a release agent and, when this was dry, wax which could be polished. The moulding, using resin and fibre-glass matting, was done in twenty-five sections, taking three weeks, with the team wearing respirators whenever the resin was being applied. Finally the sections were prised off after they had thoroughly set, turned the other way up and bolted to-gether. In this way two purposes were served. If ever a replica was built of the original, which must surely be done one day, the full details of the original shape of the ship in the ground were perma-nently recorded. At the same time, a fibre-glass 'ghost' of the 'ghost' ship was made which gives a much more immediate idea of what the

Sutton Hoo ship must have looked like to the haulers who took her up the combe above the River Deben and lowered her into her last resting-place.

The Graveney boat is different in almost every way from the Sutton Hoo ship, apart from being Anglo-Saxon. It was a small merchantman rather than a large royal vessel, it was abandoned instead of being deliberately buried, and being left in mud rather than sand, its wood survived where its metal did not. It was found, too, by accident rather than excavation. In September 1970 the Kent River Authority were digging a large drainage channel in the parish of Seasalter near the village of Graveney. In the course of this, Roy Botting, the driver of one of the mechanical excavators, struck some hard wooden timbers. He thought they looked rather like part of an old ship, and so he reported them. He did not receive a very encouraging response, but fortunately he had seen a film about the *Wasa* on television and was not to be put off. It was thanks to his persistence that the find was eventually reported to the Royal Canterbury Museum and the Canterbury Archaeological Society. They excavated the boat and in turn called in the British Museum and the National Maritime Museum at Greenwich, whose resources were put entirely at the disposal of this emergency situation by the director, Basil Greenhill. It soon became clear that the wood of the clinker-built vessel was remarkably well preserved and about seventy per cent of the vessel had survived—though discussions of possible dates ranged from the fourth to the thirteenth centuries AD. The Kent River Board therefore agreed that the drainage operation could be held up for a week and Earl Sondes, the owner of the land, gave permission for the vessel to be recorded and lifted.

After a full photographic survey had been made and a polythene shelter on scaffolding built over the vessel, the recording and lifting began. First the nine massive ribs which were fastened to the hull by wooden trenails were removed by cutting through the trenails. Then the team from the British Museum which had made the plaster cast of the Sutton Hoo ship were called in again to do the same for this, only this time it was not sand with rusty rivets in it but wet fibrous wood that had to take the plaster. Fortunately the pieces came away cleanly and easily and while it had taken three and a half days to lay the plaster, less than an hour was needed to lift the cast in nineteen pieces.

Then the boat itself had to be dismantled and lifted. It had been

OPPOSITE
Above Making a plaster cast of the remains of the Sutton Hoo ship in 1967.
Below The Graveney boat lying in the Kent River Board's drainage ditch before it was lifted and transported to the National Maritime Museum.

Gonnepowder   Shotte·of·yron   Shotte·of·Stoen·   Bowes Bowestrynge
   And·leade   Arrowes Morys pyke
   Byllys Daerts for toppis

Serpentyn		ffor Cannon		ffor port pecys		Bowes of youth
powder in		ffor di Cannon		ffor ffowlerf		Bowestrynge
barrellys		ffor Cnlueryn		ffor toppe pecys		Lyuere Arrowes
Corne powder		ffor di Cnlueryn		ffor bacellef		in sheuis
in barrellys		ffor Sakerf		Shotte of leade		Morys pykes
		ffor farcon		ffor handgonnes		Byllys
		ffor bhidy		Shotte of leade		Daertf for toppis
						in bouss

thought it might be possible to lift it out whole, but the roads across the marsh were not suitable for the necessary vehicles and equipment so it was decided to take it up piece by piece, as the Roskilde ships had been.

Anyone wandering by chance at night over that lonely piece of marsh in the bitter autumn winds would have been startled at what he suddenly saw down in that black ditch. Because the work had to be finished within the River Board's time limit, work went on well after dark. There, down in the wet mud, was the polythene structure, blazing in the bright steaming film lights, which were kept on so that work could continue after dark. Inside the polythene shelter the troglodyte team, their boots sucking and clumping through the mud, would be hard at work, numbering and labelling each separate piece of timber, matching its position next to its neighbour with bronze pins, and then lifting the strakes in turn.

The wood was still remarkably strong on the whole, and the rivets had long since vanished, so the rest of the lifting technique was simple, if extremely uncomfortable. A row of kneeling helpers would undermine each timber with their bare hands, feeling for any possible small finds in the mud, and at the same time freeing the strake from the clutch of the mud. Just before any particular length came free, a piece of plywood was slipped underneath it. Then this, with the Anglo-Saxon timber on top, was lifted on to another plank with blocks to support it at approximately the right original curvature. The piece was then carried up the bank, photographed, packed in wet plastic foam, and slipped into tubes of polythene which were duly sealed for the journey back to the Museum.

The keel, some eighteen feet (5·5 metres) long, presented perhaps the greatest problem. A small framework was made to fit this as it sat on its ridge of mud with a trench to one side. The framework was then placed over the keel, resting gently on pads of plastic foam. Then holes were made in the mud ridge underneath, through which strips of plastic foam and webbing were slid to lash the keel into its framework. When it was ready, about twenty people rocked the whole thing from side to side until it came away from the mud ridge and could be rolled carefully into the trench upside down, so that the framework would take the weight of the big tenth-century timber. It was then taken away to join the rest of the pieces in the conservation tanks at the National Maritime Museum.

Thus the vessel was successfully lifted ahead of the deadline, and the cast meant that when the time comes to reconstruct it with the

Above A contemporary illustration of the *Mary Rose*.
Below The gun deck of the *Wasa* today.

fully-conserved timbers, the exact curvature of the hull will be available from the casts.

Much useful advice was given during the operation by Ole Crumlin-Pedersen, who had shared the direction of the Roskilde Viking ships operation, and the conservation side was handled by Andrew Oddy of the British Museum Laboratory. But one of the cheering aspects of the Kentish excavation, which was outstanding for its pressure and the brutal discomfort of its working conditions (as usual the uncovered timbers had to be kept wet all the time by a spray, and neither the weather nor the setting could have been much worse), was that in charge were two extremely attractive girls, Valerie Fenwick and Angela Evans—not that it was always possible to appreciate this fact under the layers of mud.

The discussions about the date of the Graveney boat were finally settled by radio-carbon testing. The answer was that it was built about AD 900, and probably abandoned some forty years later in a rather worn condition; when found, however, it was in much worse shape, either through casual robbing of its visible upper parts or from deliberate destruction, such as King Alfred the Great ordered to be inflicted on a Danish fleet at Bamford in AD 894. In striking contrast to the Sutton Hoo ship, the inside of the hull was to all intents empty; virtually the only finds were some hops, a few pieces of stone, and a bit of pottery which had probably been washed into it. Had it originally been a coaster bringing building materials or local salt to London, and later converted into a mere barge after some accident to its keel? We will probably never know.

One thing is certain, though. Like many second finds from one particular period, as happened when the Cheops ship joined the Dahshur vessels, and the Roskilde fleet the Gokstad and Oseberg finds, it has modified previous generalisations. The usual idea of a vessel of that period of the Dark Ages is of a sweeping double-ended shape with curving stem and stern—but the Graveney ship had a definite heel at its stern. So now we know for certain that this feature was not just an artistic eccentricity in certain carvings. And the National Maritime Museum at Greenwich will also in due course have an Anglo-Saxon craft on display, even if not quite as magnificent as the Viking ships in Scandinavia.

Above all, and perhaps most important, there is now in Britain a nucleus of experienced ship excavators. Next time a comparable craft is found, there will not be quite the same impulse to say, as C. W. Phillips said, 'Oh, my godfathers!'

A ship from a picture stone in Gotland, Sweden, of the early Viking period, with a hull shape which may have been something like that of the Graveney boat.

10

The Wasa, Mary Rose and Amsterdam: War at Sea

August 10th 1628 was a Sunday and a fine afternoon in Stockholm. Sweden and the capital city were full of excitement because King Gustav II's plans to acquire a powerful new fleet were about to be realised in part. The comic-opera status which had made General Wallenstein 'Grand Admiral of the Baltic' without a single ship to command was progressively ending: the King had ordered four warships to be built to counter the Austrian Emperor's threat to invade Scandinavia in the course of what is now called the Thirty Years War, and one of them was about to go on its maiden voyage. Since Sweden's own experience of large warships was limited, this particular vessel, the *Wasa*, named after the Swedish ruling family, was designed by a Dutchman and commanded by a Dane.

Just after vespers the new vessel was warped downstream and then set her topsails, a foresail and mizzen. About five o'clock, opposite the island of Beckholmen, she was struck by a sudden squall. Over to port she heeled, the water came in through her gunports and in plain view of the crowds on shore, with her many flags still flying, she went to the bottom. Though at the time this was a national disaster which dismayed all Sweden, and the name of the *Wasa* became at once notorious, she was, like the Kyrenia ship, to have a second chapter in her life which was to make her even more famous.

The *Wasa* disaster was the direct result of an all-too-familiar process that even in 1628 had been going on for nearly three thousand years—the Naval Arms Race. It had certainly started by at least the thirteenth century BC, for there is a record of the battle of Suppiluliuma when the Hittites defeated a fleet from Cyprus

An impression of how the *Wasa* looked on her maiden voyage. She sank too soon for any contemporary record of her appearance to be made.

before conquering that island. Many other naval battles are also mentioned from this time, and one account even describes a fleet of 150 ships from the city of Ugarit which was in the service of the Hittites.

Not long after that comes the oldest surviving illustration of a naval battle, on the side of the Temple of Medinet-Habu in Egypt (cf. Chapter 1); and that relief contains a small but significant detail. One of the invading ships, quite different from the Egyptian ones, has a small protruding extension at the foot of its bow. It could well have been larger in actual fact; but perhaps because it was strange to the Egyptian sculptor of the scene, he may not have given it much emphasis. There was no question of rams of this kind being used in warfare at this time (1190 BC or so), but rams of a sort did occur in considerable numbers for quite a different reason. At that time, harbours, if they existed at all, were little more than a protecting natural rock, perhaps flattened a little to make a quay, like the one still to be seen on the island of Arwad, north of Byblos. The majority of voyages in those days ended on a beach, and a ram sticking out from bow or stern was an excellent means of protecting the hull when beaching.

We do not know the name of the brilliant naval strategist who first saw that such a device could be used offensively against another ship, instead of just protecting one's own. Nor do we know when it was first used, but most likely it was some time after 1000 BC, because Homer never mentions the idea. When it did happen, warships ceased to be mere troop transports and became instead what Lionel Casson, the great American naval historian, has vividly called 'man-driven torpedoes'. The implications of this new development were far-reaching, because ships now had to be built quite differently, both to deliver and to sustain the shock of ramming. The Greeks tended to favour a rather stubby type of ram with a number of prongs, the Phoenicians a long needle-like affair. Then another man of imagination thought up the two-banked warship, to be followed about 600 BC by perhaps the most characteristic of ancient ram warships, the 'trieris' or 'trireme', in which the addition of an outrigger enabled a third bank of oars to give added speed and manoeuvrability.

The name of the next revolutionary genius we actually know: it was Demetrius the 'Besieger', one of the rulers who took over parts of Alexander the Great's empire, whose coins helped to date the Kyrenia ship. He turned the one- or two-man-per-oar crew into a multiple unit. Now began something like the Dreadnought Race of the early twentieth century, or the building of the last vast Japanese battleships of the Second World War. More men were added to each oar until at the end of the third century BC we reach the most fantastic of all ancient warships, the 'forty' of Ptolemy IV which was probably a catamaran or double hull, manned by four thousand oarsmen divided between three banks of oars, with from five to eight men on each oar.

But already another weapon was on its way, the missile hurler. Demetrius the 'Besieger' had also pioneered the use of catapults on ships, and the Romans subtly adapted this to suit their military strength by using them to hurl grapnels which then hauled their enemies alongside. It is not difficult to see in this a memory of the '*corvus*' or raven which had made up for their landsmen's inexperience when first faced with the sea-hardened Carthaginians: it was a gangplank with a spike at the end, secured to a pole and tackles on the bow, and when dropped onto the enemy craft it enabled a force of marines to rush over and board their opponents.

Phoenician warship with ram.

As early as 190 BC, the last new naval weapon to be invented in the ancient world was introduced by an ingenious admiral from Rhodes called Pausistratus. This was the fire-pot. It consisted of a funnel-shaped iron container holding inflammable liquid, which was slung on the end of a long pole. The idea was to tip its contents onto the enemy's deck by means of a chain attached to the lip of the funnel, or to make him sheer off and so become vulnerable to a ram attack.

This was in a sense the part-ancestor of the deadly secret weapon of the post-Roman Byzantine navy—'Greek fire'. We still do not know exactly what it was, but it was probably some form of petroleum product, which was poured into a long wooden tube lined with bronze called a siphon. The siphon was fitted at its inboard end with an air-pump. When operated, this turned the apparatus into a very effective and terrifying flame-thrower. The same 'Greek fire' was also used in missiles which were hurled at the enemy, to explode into flames on impact.

These almost twentieth-century devices seem curiously ahead of their time, like the rockets which were part of late eighteenth-century artillery equipment. Yet they were to be superseded by a cruder but nevertheless effective weapon which was to rule the seas for almost four centuries—the naval cannon.

In 1346, King Edward III used not only the deadly longbow but also some 'bombards' to enable his outnumbered army to defeat the vast array of French knights at Crécy. There is a record of an 'artificium longum et ingens' being used on a Genoese ship twenty-seven years before this, but most people now agree that this was still a tube for 'Greek fire'. So the distinction of being the first man recorded to have used guns on board ship probably belongs to the Frenchman Louis de Male, who was sent to attack Antwerp from the sea ten years before the Battle of Crécy.

At first both hand-guns and cannon were used on ships very much as bows and arrows had been before—to send down a hail of missiles from the 'castles' at bow and stern, or 'fighting tops' on the mast, to clear the enemy deck preparatory to boarding. But then as cannon grew bigger and more efficient, a problem arose: the more cannon that were placed in the waist of a ship, the more top-heavy and unstable the vessel became. The answer was a brilliant idea on a par with the ram, the 'corvus', and 'Greek fire'—the gunport. Sometime between 1500 and 1540, someone had the notion of cutting apertures in the side of the ship for cannon to fire through;

when not in use they could be covered with flaps to keep out the water. This meant that cannon could be sited much lower and nearer the ship's centre of gravity, and so there could be more and larger ones. But making holes in the sides of ships, however useful otherwise, can be a disadvantage too, if they are left open at the wrong moment. And this both the *Wasa* and *Mary Rose*, amongst many others, were to demonstrate only too well.

The *Wasa's* second chapter of existence we owe largely to the absence of a small and undistinguished creature, the *teredo navalis* or shipworm, which harassed wooden shipbuilders for so many centuries. One of its characteristics is that it cannot live in the relatively fresh waters of the Baltic. This had two results in particular. One was that the *Wasa's* structure was preserved. The other was that a Swede called Anders Franzen, inspired by this, was encouraged to search for her. He was a man who combined archive research with underwater investigation, and concentrated on the period of perhaps Sweden's greatest impact on European affairs, the seventeenth century.

His research into previous salvage attempts convinced Franzen that the *Wasa* lay about 110 feet (33·5 metres) down somewhere off Beckholmen. He shaded in all the areas of this depth on a chart of the harbour and started searching by boat with a grapnel. When this brought up something interesting (and not just the many cables which criss-crossed the bottom of Stockholm harbour) he used a device, the sounding lead, which goes back at least to before 2000 BC, because some ship models from the ancient Egyptian tomb of a courtier called Meketre show one of the crew holding one. Franzen's was a rather more sophisticated version with an automatically-operated punch in the end, and this brought up at will samples of whatever he dropped it on.

His crucial moment came when a single area started yielding successive samples of black oak. The next step was to bring in the Royal Swedish Navy's diver-training service. Their report was simple: the *Wasa* was there all right, sunk in clay but more or less upright, and extraordinarily well preserved. Neither weather, worms, or even the anchors that had been dragged over her seemed to have done much harm. In fact much the greatest damage had come from earlier salvage attempts.

These seventeenth-century rescue operations are a remarkable story in themselves. The first hopeful was given permission to start work only three days after the disaster. He was an Englishman called Ian Bulmer with the impressive title 'Engineer to His Majesty the King of England', and he did live up to this in one important way: he raised nothing, but he got the wreck on to an even keel, which was going to mean a lot to future salvors. After various attempts, the next serious effort was made by a Swede and a German, von Treileben and Peckell, who were experts in the use of diving bells. They got to work in 1663 and contemporary accounts give a good picture of the conditions under which they worked. After putting on a watertight leather suit, the diver climbed into the lead bell, four foot two inches (1·27 metres) high. Hanging twenty inches (45 cms) under the bell was a square piece of lead for the diver to stand on. A line attached to a ring on top of the bell then lowered the diver to the bottom, 110 feet (33·4 metres) down. The water by this time had risen almost up to the diver's neck inside the bell and the remaining air was compressed into a quarter of the bell's volume. There the diver got to work, mainly by feel, with an assortment of hooks, pincers, prongs and nets on the end of long poles and, most important, his signalling rope which ran under the rim of the bell and up to the surface to give warning when he wanted to be raised.

Later the British astronomer Edmund Halley is credited with inventing a device by which fresh air was supplied to the divers in the bell by means of wooden casks. Another Englishman, Edwin Maulde, also took advantage of his experience gained on the *Wasa* to go and search in 1666 in another diving bell for the notorious Armada galleon sunk in Tobermory Bay in Scotland.

What von Treileben and the others achieved under these conditions was quite remarkable. Besides creating a confusion of slashed rigging, torn decks, fallen timber and anchor chains to hamper future salvors, they not only managed to lift the cannon on the upper deck but even to get them up from below decks. It was fortunate for posterity that they concentrated on them rather than the other contents of the ship; when Franzen re-found the wreck nearly three hundred years later, he came on what was virtually a 'village under the sea', a sea-faring community with all its possessions, clothes, cooking gear and furniture, cut off in a moment and sealed in by black muddiness at the bottom of Stockholm harbour.

By 1958 a specially formed committee had reported that it was feasible to salvage the *Wasa* and that the attempt should go ahead. The story goes that one of the first single objects the modern divers brought up was a block of seventeenth-century butter. In the sunshine of Stockholm harbour it soon began to melt. This was

The *Wasa* being towed shorewards on a concrete pontoon inside the aluminium framework of the building which now houses her.

long before the complicated and impressive conservation equipment of later stages had been organised. 'What shall we do with it?' they asked anxiously. 'Take it straight back to the sea bed,' was the answer. 'It has survived three hundred years there—it ought to be all right for a day or two more.'

It was decided that the first step in salvaging the ship itself should be to move her to shallower water. To do this, six tunnels were first dug under the hull by water-jets combined with mud suction pumps. The divers crept down these tunnels in complete darkness, the pipe of the pump-jet between their legs. Above their heads was not only the possibly unsound hull of the wreck but the many tons of stone ballast in her lower holds. It was certainly not a job for anyone with weak nerves. But eventually the Swedish Royal Navy divers achieved it, emulating the bravery of their ancient diving-bell predecessors, so that six great six-inch steel wires could be passed under the keel. These were attached to two salvage pontoons, one on each side of the sunken warship. In August 1959 the technique was put to the test for the first time. No one knew if

Some of the finds
from the *Wasa* in the
course of conservation.

the *Wasa* would collapse inward, disintegrate, refuse to move or
co-operate in any way in her start to a new life. In fact she behaved
perfectly and rose neatly out of the fifteen-foot deep (4·3-metre)
trench which she had made for herself on the bottom. There
followed a series of lifts and gentle bumps as she was raised a
few feet at a time; then she was towed landwards until she grounded,
and the process was repeated.

By September 1959 she lay in only fifty feet (fifteen metres) of
water, and a new stage began. Now the divers sealed the fatal gunports and every other opening they could find, repaired broken
timbers and replaced nails that had rusted away until once more
she was more or less what she had been 333 years before, a watertight hull.

Now she was ready for the most dramatic moment of all, the
surfacing. This was to be achieved by means of special hydraulic
jacks placed on the inward sides of the two pontoons. To these
were attached new nine-inch (22-cm) wires under the hull, and, for
additional lift, four collapsible rubber pontoons were put under her
stern. On April 24th the rubber pontoons were inflated and the

hydraulic jacks began to heave in the wires, and for the first time her superstructure broke surface. The two carved wooden heads on the foremast 'bitts' rightly seemed to wear a look of astonishment as they looked out across Stockholm harbour. Any leaks could be more easily stopped up now, and as the pumps cleared the water and mud from her 'tween-decks she rose up slowly and steadily until by May 4th she was fully afloat, on her own keel but with a slight list to port. In this condition she was towed into dry dock and over the concrete platform which was to be the eventual floor of the Wasa Museum. By now, too, there had been begun the continuous spraying and elaborate conservation processes which will have to go on for many, many years, if not indefinitely.

This was not only one of the most remarkable salvage operations ever achieved; in the course of it, many pieces of splendidly carved wood were recovered, as well as more prosaic things, from boots to tankards. Just as the metal hoard of the Cape Gelidonya ship had done in its way, so this one source vastly increased our knowledge and appreciation of Swedish seventeenth-century woodcarving and at the same time laid open to the public the earliest specifically named and known ship in existence.

The ship which ran ashore on Bulverhithe beach near Hastings on January 26th 1749, had both similarities to and differences from the *Wasa*. Like the *Wasa*, the *Amsterdam* was also on her maiden voyage, and, like her, may one day have a second chapter to her life in the twentieth century after a major salvage operation. But there the parallels end. To start with, she was no warship but a merchantman, one of the big well-armed ones with which the 'Gentlemen Seventeen', or ruling committee of the Dutch East India Company, built up their great trading empire. She was built in 1748 in the city from which she took her name and was due to sail in November of that year to Batavia in the Dutch East Indies. But Captain-Lieutenant William Klump was unlucky. Twice he met head winds and had to put back so that she only finally sailed in January 1749. Quite apart from the weather, this had other unfortunate repercussions amongst the 203 sailors, 127 soldiers and five passengers we know were on board. At that time it was the habit to eke out a crew with any available jailbirds. Once on board they obviously could not be allowed any shore leave, so the *Amsterdam*'s quota of convicts had three months in which to go down with any diseases they had brought with them, before they even began their long voyage half way round the world.

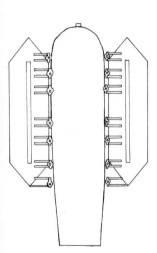

The hull shape of the *Wasa*, with the two pontoons and their hydraulic lifting jacks on either side of her.

As it was, a fortnight after her third sailing, she had only reached Pevensey Bay, off Sussex, when she struck a shoal and lost her rudder. Klump anchored off Bexhill, hoping eventually to reach Portsmouth for repairs. But by Sunday, January 26th, in an extremely exposed anchorage, with perhaps eighty of his crew down with yellow fever, and no proper means of steering, he must have known his chances were poor. So he raised anchor and let the ship drive towards the mouth of a creek with a river running into it at Bulverhithe. There she ran aground. Although most people on board seem to have been rescued, this must have been more by luck than good judgement, because most of the crew who were not too feeble from yellow fever had got in amongst the twelve thousand bottles of wine in the cargo and were hopelessly drunk. Their example was not long in being followed by the rescuers from Hastings, who had been alerted by the ship firing her cannon as a distress signal. By Monday at least a thousand wreckers were at work on the beach. The Dutch soldiers tried to protect the wreck, and to their dubious aid came a company of English Foot, recently returned from fighting Bonnie Prince Charlie at Culloden, who were described by one eye-witness as 'the greatest thieves I ever saw'. But this was where chance favoured the twentieth century rather than the eighteenth, just as it did some two months later when the salvage engineer in charge, a certain appropriately-named Mr Nutt, blew himself up trying to blast a way into the surviving cargo. By February 4th the ship had sunk into the silt of the river-mouth so much that, although the treasure chests of silver had been rescued, it was impossible to get at the main part of the cargo. By February 11th the main hatches could not be opened. By March she was completely covered at high water and by the 11th of that month the Dutch East India Company gave up her salvage as a bad job.

The masts and rigging, the gilded and decorated poop and the fo'c'sle could not have lasted long against the battering of the sea and probably she soon became what she is still today, an outline of a ship in jagged black timbers which appears above the sand when the tide is really low.

Luck again intervened when, in the nineteenth century, the Hastings Corporation put a sewage discharge pipe a short way away from her. This discouraged bathing and beach play near her, and though various salvage attempts were made, it was not until the Corporation decided to build a new sewer outfall discharging two miles out to sea that any dramatic change in her condition occurred.

The *Amsterdam* at low tide on Hastings beach.

There happened to be in local charge of the company laying the new sewer an amateur archaeologist who thought it would be interesting to explore the wreck rather more thoroughly than could be done with hand tools. So in July 1969 he started using mechanical excavators on the ship to see what, if anything, remained inside the outline of the hull. The excavators were able to get much further down into the ship than anyone had since the eighteenth century. Major finds included five bronze cannon and many bottles of the red wine which had consoled the original crew—though now after years of contamination through somewhat inadequate stoppers it would be a brave man who would drink the contents today. Other smaller finds included musket balls, a smoothing iron, heather brushes in an extraordinarily good state of preservation, a charming lady's fan, a cake of tallow, a wooden shoe and various other things.

This could hardly be called a scientific excavation because no record was made of the position of the finds before they were lifted. Fortunately, however, the company got in touch with the

Council for Nautical Archaeology through its local representative, Bill Wilkes, and from then on a number of properly scientific studies of the ship were made under the direction of Peter Marsden of the Guildhall Museum, London, with the support of the C.N.A., the BBC 2 programme *Chronicle*, and various commercial organisations. The studies consisted of a sonar search done at high tide when the wreck was covered with water, a metal detector survey, probing, and excavation done at low tide when the ship was uncovered.

The excavation part of the operation nearly always provided a good sight for the many spectators, as the lowest tides giving the longest working periods always seem to occur at dusk or dawn. Once the falling tide uncovered the ship a race would start, to make holes on each side of the ship's outline to establish the amount and state of the hull remaining. As the pumps sucked desperately to keep the holes water-free for as long as possible, Peter Marsden and his team of archaeologists clambered about in the thick mud, plotting, recording and surveying in the steaming glow of the film lights, collecting small finds, making notes, all the time racing against the turning tide. All too soon the water would return, making the sides of the trenches collapse; the vehicles would race landwards, and once more the wreck would be back in its grip of sand and mud.

What these excavations and the other studies revealed is that the hull of the *Amsterdam* is still perhaps three-quarters complete. Much of its contents is also still on board, less of course the treasure of silver which was the first target of the eighteenth-century salvors and looters. The *Amsterdam* therefore is a remarkable historical document, coming in date as she does between her two nearest rivals, the *Wasa* and HMS *Victory*, and being, unlike them, a merchant ship.

To salvage her would be a considerable task, since like the Graveney boat most of the iron bolts holding her timbers together have rusted away, but her timbers are in remarkably fine and hard condition. There is also an occasion to hand which might well prompt the effort needed to salve her, for 1975 is the seven hundredth anniversary of her home port and name town, Amsterdam, and the Dutch are some of the greatest salvage and towing experts in the world. It has been suggested that a cofferdam should be built round her with laboratories and so on over the top. Then she would be excavated and fastened with slings to the dam, and finally the whole structure would be floated off at high tide and towed back to

Holland with the hull slung underneath, to form eventually another *Wasa*-type museum. It would be a fitting tribute to the skills and maritime enterprise of the Dutch East India Company, and a chance for the first time to see what the interior of an East Indiaman looked like on a life-size scale.

The story of the *Mary Rose* is far closer to that of the *Wasa* than the *Amsterdam*. The *Mary Rose* was a warship and, like the *Wasa*, she heeled over and sank before the horrified eyes of crowds on shore when water entered her lower gunports. But what is so special about the *Mary Rose* is that she was one of the first warships ever to have gunports, so she occupies a particular place in the long and often agonising and disastrous history of the Naval Arms Race.

The *Mary Rose* was built for King Henry VIII at Portsmouth in 1509. This four-masted carrack of some six hundred tons was revolutionary because she was the first English warship to have the land siege-artillery of the day as her maindeck armament. With this, in 1512, she defeated the French Admiral's ship *Grande Louise* off Brest. Then in 1536 she was rebuilt, her displacement increased by a hundred tons, and there was the vital introduction of gunports. Though in a sense she was one of the ancestors of the 'broadside' ship which was to bear the brunt of sea-warfare for the next three hundred years, not surprisingly at this early stage she would have seemed a strangely experimental bag of tricks to Nelson, with her high bow and stern castles and her mixed armament of culverins, culverin bastards, demi-cannon, cannon royal and breech-loading bombards, compared to the neat rows of 24- and 32-pounders of the Napoleonic wars. Nevertheless, she so obviously showed the potential of being able to increase the amount of artillery by siting the weight of it low down in the ship and firing through gunports, that four years later Henry VIII ordered the *Great Harry*, his thousand-ton flagship, to be rebuilt in the same way.

Sadly for the king, he was to see for himself that this new piece of ship design had its drawbacks as well as its advantages. In 1545 the Battle of Portsmouth took place, a naval encounter known to few Englishmen, but a familiar part of French schoolchildren's history since it is classed as a French victory. When the French fleet appeared off the Isle of Wight, the English fleet sailed out to meet them. Henry VIII, after dining with his admirals and captains aboard the *Great Harry* and 'giving them comfortable words', went ashore to watch the ensuing battle from Southsea castle. With him, amongst others, was the wife of the admiral in the *Mary Rose*, Sir George Carewe. But even before any exchange of shots took place, the English suffered their first disaster. The *Mary Rose* heeled over, her improperly secured cannon added their momentum to the movement, and, like the *Wasa*, in a few minutes she and her admiral were gone. Only three dozen of the seven hundred or so people on board are said to have survived.

Since she sank in only fifty feet (fifteen metres) of water, the tops of her masts probably remained visible at first, and there was confidence she could be salvaged. Some guns, yards, and sails were indeed rescued. Then, like the *Wasa* and the *Amsterdam*, she began to settle into mud and obscurity. This was interrupted between 1836 and 1840 when John Deane, inventor of the first really usable diving helmet, was asked by some Gosport fishermen to clear an obstruction on the bottom which was fouling their nets. This he managed, recovering some more guns and other objects in the process, but in so doing he made it much more difficult for the man who was to be to the *Mary Rose* what Anders Franzen had been to the *Wasa*.

Virtually no surface sign was left of the wreck when Alexander McKee first became interested in finding it in 1965. For a long time Alex McKee, diver, author and naval historian, had little to go on but two pieces of paper and his own prickly determination. One piece of paper was a chart he had found in the Admiralty Hydrographic Department which showed the actual site of the *Mary Rose*, as opposed to the one that legend had by now given it. The other was a brown sonar trace which according to McKee confirmed the presence there of the hull under the mud. It was hard at that stage for those not directly involved to accept that the smudged W-shape on the trace could be the hull of the *Mary Rose*. But McKee never faltered and gradually his helpers grew in numbers. Margaret Rule, an experienced archaeologist and keeper of Fishbourne Roman Villa, learnt to skin-dive so that she could see for herself the evidence on the bottom and add the skills of a trained excavator to the operation. Shipwright Maurice Young was particularly useful for identifying whereabouts on the hull the first odd finds of wood might have come from, as was W. O. B. Majer, an authority on medieval ships.

Diving conditions were appalling. Standard visibility was about six inches (fifteen cms), and working in the pitch-dark trench they excavated to find the hull was not for the claustrophobic. But the thick sediment which the double tides of the Solent swept to and

Lifting the second iron gun from the *Mary Rose* in November 1971.

fro had its advantages; the wreck lay under some fifteen feet (4·57 metres) of it, which was useful, to say the least, in an area where anchors and trawls were frequently dragged and the Isle of Wight ferries raised a mud storm every time they passed. Nevertheless the divers, who came from the City of Portsmouth Fire Brigade, the Services, and local branches of the British Sub Aqua Club, fought, dug, and felt their way on. On the surface they received more and more help from the Portsmouth City Corporation, *Chronicle* and various firms. In 1969 they had struck hard wood, and various wooden objects began to be brought up. Then came a stroke of luck. They found a gun, and what a gun it was—an eight-foot-long breech-loading bombard. Not only was it of the right Tudor period, but it still had in it an iron ball, oakum wadding, and remains of the black powder that was going to hurl the missile against the French on that far-off day of 1545. It was also of a hitherto unknown design; instead of being made of a series of iron bars welded together and secured by iron hoops, it consisted of a single sheet of metal bent

round in a circle, welded down the join, and then ringed with rein-
forcing hoops.

By the end of the 1973 season the excavators had uncovered 110
feet (34 metres) of one side of the wreck and gone down deep enough
to tell from the shape of the tumble-home, or curve of the ship's side,
that there was perhaps thirty feet (nine metres) of depth of hull
remaining. Moreover, thanks to the otherwise tiresome sediment,
the wood, like that of the *Amsterdam*, seemed to be in remarkably
good condition; not only did it still show the marks of the Tudor
shipwright's tools, but when it was planed, shavings came off, and
when it was sawed, actual sawdust appeared. On the starboard side
were the collapsed remains of the stern castle, built in a hitherto
unvisualised way. And trapped among the wreckage of it were not
only ready-use caches of shot but combs, a thimble, thread spools,
and other objects from a sailor's 'ditty box', a hint that the hull
might be as rich in its contents as the *Wasa* and *Amsterdam*.

There is therefore a good chance, if the money can be raised,
that one day the *Mary Rose* may emulate the *Wasa* and rise to the
surface, and in so doing take over the title of the earliest lifted
specifically-named ship, as well as solving many problems about a
critical moment in naval architecture. If she does eventually find a
home in a museum, she may well have alongside her a worthy,
if not so complete, consort; for a few miles away, on the mud
of the River Hamble, lie the burnt and battered remains of the
greatest English ship of the fifteenth century, the *Grace Dieu*.
Built in 1418 for King Henry V, she was ready too late for the war
she was designed to take part in. Being well before the period of
gunports, her 1,400 tons succumbed to a quite different but also
common threat to sailors—fire. Towed up the River Hamble with
only a small maintenance crew on board after the end of the war
with France, she was struck by lightning in 1434 and burnt out down
to the waterline.

Her structural and tactical affinities are not with the *Mary Rose*,
but with a craft found while Bremen harbour on the River Weser
in Germany was being deepened in 1962. This is a vessel known
as the 'Bremen Cog', which seems as though it was never completed
but swept away, wrecked and abandoned during building, perhaps
by a sudden flood. Like the *Grace Dieu*, the 'Bremen Cog' has a
mixture of clinker and carvel building in her construction. As a
type, the cog seems to have been heavy, flat-bottomed, and high-
sided; this gave a greater cargo capacity than the faster, lighter,

purely clinker-built vessels of the Vikings. In warfare, despite the handicap of poor manoeuvrability, the cog had height and a strong platform for archers, hand-gun firers and missile-droppers in any encounter with a long-ship.

So gradually a picture is emerging, through actual remains, of how different types of vessels evolved in Europe, from the virtually open boats of the Vikings to craft capable of sailing round the world. There are many gaps and problems still, but at least the whole subject is rather more detailed than it was fifteen years ago.

As one looks at this new knowledge, one cannot help thinking that the Naval Arms Race, which forms so much a part of it, is a reflection also of the folly of the human race. Endless grief, pain and personal suffering are submerged in it. It is perhaps a consolation that out of this should come also some small benefit—a greater knowledge of history, of the skill of the shipwrights who built the vessels, of the lives of the sailors who lived aboard, and how the vessels themselves were sailed and used.

A medieval seal from Stralsund, Germany, showing a 'cog' with its typical high sides and straight extremities.

THE FUTURE

A ship must have sunk every day, somewhere, somehow, ever since man first took to the sea; so George Bass has said, and rightly. Yet we have scarcely touched this great underwater store of history. We have no Cretan, no early Phoenician and no Etruscan ship, and no classical Mediterranean warship of any sort. In northern Europe an early medieval 'hulk' would be a useful find, as would a more or less complete Spanish Armada wreck, such as *La Trinidad Valenciera* may turn out to be in Glenagivney Bay off Donegal, in Ireland.

Up to now, chance has played the largest part in existing finds, and the fact that amphorae cargoes make distinctive landmarks on the sea-bed has given a distinct bias to the nature of Mediterranean discoveries. But various technical developments may soon change all this. It is already possible to work at depths well below hitherto normal diving levels, where wrecks should be undisturbed by vandals and weather alike. Furthermore, below a certain depth, the teredo ceases to find acceptable living conditions; so below 200 metres and before reaching 2,000 metres, where a borer clam called the *Xylophaga* exists, there is likely to be a destruction-free zone.

More effective mud-piercing sonar should be available, and it is not inconceivable that one day we may be able to locate wood under the bottom of the sea by some means as yet unthought of.

Then there are area-searches, which instead of concentrating on one find search very closely over an area where there must be wrecks, like the site of a sea battle. One of the most remarkable has taken place in the now reclaimed areas of the Zuider Zee in Holland. In the course of draining the North East Polder no fewer than 156 wrecks were found, and a highly-organised programme of examining and recording them has been carried out by G. van der Heide.

We also urgently need to preserve actual modern craft, especially those with long traditions behind them, and to make full film, photographic and sound recordings of how they are made, before the traditional craftsmen who build them disappear.

One thing is certain in this field. There is much to be done and much still to be found out.

BOOKS FOR FURTHER READING

If you want to read more about this subject in detail, the following books all have full references to the original sources. You can also subscribe to *The International Journal of Nautical Archaeology*, which is published twice yearly at £5.00 an issue. It contains up-to-date articles and reports on the latest developments in the subject, and is published by the Seminar Press Ltd, 24–28 Oval Road, London NW1, England.

BASS, G. *Archaeology under water*. New York: Praeger Publishers, Inc., 1966
————. *A history of seafaring*. New York: Walker & Company, 1972
BASS, G., et al. *Cape Gelidonya : A Bronze Age shipwreck*. Transactions series. Philadelphia, Pa.: American Philosophical Society, 1967
CASSON, L. *Ancient mariners*. New York: The Macmillan Company, 1959
————. *Ships and seamanship in the ancient world*. Princeton, N.J.: Princeton University Press, 1971
FRANZEN, G. *Great ship Vasa. Famous museum series*. New York: Hastings House, Publishers, Inc., 1971
LANDSTROM, B. *Ships of the Pharaohs*. New York: Doubleday & Company, Inc., 1970
LEWIS, D. *We, the navigators*. Honolulu, Hawaii: The University Press of Hawaii, 1972
McKEE, A. *History under the sea*. New York: E. P. Dutton & Co., Inc., 1969
MORRISON, J. S., and WILLIAMS, R. T. *Greek oared ships*. New York: Cambridge University Press, 1968
RACKL, H. W. *Diving into the past*. New York: Charles Scribner's Sons, 1968
SAWYER, P. *The age of the Vikings*. 2nd ed. New York: St. Martin's Press, Inc., 1972
SUGGS, R. T. *Island civilisations of Polynesia*. New York: The New American Library, Inc., 1960
THROCKMORTON, P. *Shipwrecks and archaeology*. Boston, Mass.: Little, Brown and Company, 1970

INDEX